Dowio

Unusualore

Ron Brown

Polar Bear Press
Toronto

distributed by
North 49 Books
35 Prince Andrew Place
Toronto, Ontario M3C 2H2
416 449-4000

Canadian Cataloguing in Publication Data

Brown, Ron, 1945-
 Downtown Ontario; Unusual Main Streets to Explore

includes index
ISBN 1-896757-24-3 (v. 1)

1. Steets – Ontario – History   2. Ontario – History, Local I. Title

FC3062.b792 2003   917.3   C2003-900569-0
F1057.8.B792 2003

Printed in Canada

Front cover photos:
Top Left: St Mary's
Top Right: Port Perry
Middle Left: Goderich
Middle Right:Merrickville
Lower Right: St Mary's

Table of Contents

Introduction

Welcome to Ontario's most unusual main streets

In earliest times, a city's downtown developed around its most important function, usually a marketplace where sellers would bring produce to trade. Gradually, more permanent shops of artisans and traders would appear around the square and, as the community grew, would extend along the roads that led to the square.

During the Renaissance, squares were designed as part of enlightened town planning, for aesthetic as well as functional reasons. In administrative centres, these would usually include the offices of the village councils and bureaucrats. But no matter where or when town centres appeared, they were the heart of the community.

In Canada, other factors determined where the main street would be and how it would appear. Newfoundland's towns, for example, had no main streets. Houses were built where space permitted around a rocky cove. Goods were shipped in from merchants in the cities and sold through a local seller.

In Quebec, long thin farm lots meant that houses were at close intervals along the roads. The centre of the Quebec community was invariably the Roman Catholic Church, and the nearest farm lots would often be divided to accommodate the taverns and the shops.

Prairie main streets were usually a device of the railway builders and consisted of a wide main street leading away from the back door of the station, largely to impress potential investors arriving by train.

Ontario main streets tended to develop with commerce in mind. The first town sites were laid out by British surveyors, and were situated in the centre of each township with typical disregard to geography. Indeed, Ontario is dotted with many such "paper towns" that, while laid out on paper, never grew. Then, through the 1800s, as settlement spread, towns developed around the facilities that the pioneers most needed, like mill sites, harbours and taverns, and around the shops at key crossroads locations.

Ontario's main street architecture, in the beginning, was simple, consisting of free-standing wooden buildings, sometimes two storeys high and either sporting a front gable or a false front facade. As towns grew and the lumber supply dwindled, brickyards were opened to supply material for new stores and shops. Where bedrock was near the surface, stones became the building material of choice. In a few areas, even field stones were called into use.

Individual stores gave way to the commercial block, which contained as few as two or three store fronts, or as many as a dozen. As the century progressed, architecture became more experimental, with the simple Georgian giving way to Italianate, neo-classical, Queen Anne and Romanesque styles. Such devices as parapets, pilasters, two-toned brick, domes, dormers and fancy gables were all meant to make the main street more appealing.

The range of functions tended to be similar from one town to the next. Besides the stores, there were usually two or more taverns, a post office and a town hall. Because of the variety of religious denominations in Ontario, churches seldom occupied places of prominence on the main street, although they were rarely far away.

Nor were railway stations likely to dominate the main street as they did on the prairies. When the railways began to make their way into Ontario from the 1850s to the 1880s, most towns were already established. And because land tended to be cheaper farther from the centre of town, stations were often located on the outskirts.

For many decades Ontario's main streets remained the heart of the town. People gathered to gossip, to watch parades or to buy their necessities.

But main streets had one ultimately fatal flaw. They were of necessity pedestrian-oriented. Shoppers would walk from their homes along one of the side streets, or come by horse and tie up at a hitching post. They were most decidedly not for cars. When the automobile burst upon the scene in the 1920s, drivers found there was no place to park. A car or two would take up the space in front of an entire store, and main streets began to get congested.

The suburban phenomenon of the 1950s seemed to solve that with the invention of the suburban shopping mall. These were, of course, parking lots first, with the stores lined along the perimeter. As housing moved farther away from the old downtown and as shopping centres evolved into regional malls and eventually into big box power centres, the old main streets became forgotten backwaters. Family businesses shut down in the face of franchises and retail giants. Shoppers flocked to the biggest stores offering the best bargains.

A few main streets have managed to survive in the face of it all. In some cases competition has been less severe, and the business community has been more progressive. Others have reinvented themselves by finding a specialty or niche market, while still others have simply given up, leaving stores to close and sidewalks to grow over with weeds.

To help counter the deadly impact, Business Improvement Associations began to spring up on Ontario's main streets. They would coordinate promotion and undertake streetscaping to try to lure shoppers back downtown. Often LACACs would get involved as well. These local architectural advisory committees would identify buildings of special historic or architectural value and encourage the local council to designate them under Ontario's Heritage Act. Unfortunately, this act is among the world's weakest and designation oddly doesn't prevent demolition. It does, however, improve awareness and sometimes makes owners eligible for special grants and loans to preserve the heritage of the building. As some business owners have found, heritage usually pays.

Being one of Canada's largest provinces, Ontario can claim to have approximately 1000 "main streets." These might range in size from a handful of shops clustered in the centre of a village to several blocks of solid brick buildings. And, even though the architecture and functions may be similar, no two are really the same.

In fact, some are decidedly different, even unusual.

There are those with more imaginative layouts, such as Goderich with its eight-sided "square," or Kapuskasing, a planned town in the northern bush with its famous main street circle. Some main streets, such as that in Petrolia, went through forgotten booms and were blessed with extraordinary architecture. Other main streets are different because they have retained a heritage from a much earlier period, such as Barriefield or Maitland, or from an unusual event in their past, such as the gold and silver rushes that gave rise to Kirkland Lake and Cobalt, respectively. Still others had their peculiar configuration determined by a quirk of nature.

This volume guides the reader across Ontario to explore Ontario's fifty most unusual main streets.

Ron Brown
Toronto, Ontario

 Alton

... a main street from the past...

Sprawling along the waters of Shaw's Creek, a tributary of the historic Credit River, Alton is a rapidly expanding community with a residential future, and a main street from the past.

The community began with the arrival of Thomas Russell in 1834. But it wasn't until 1851 that the site received its first grist mill, that of Shrigley and Farr, and its first general store. A busy commercial core developed along Queen St, parallel to the river. There were several stores, a carriage factory constructed of stone, and the Dixie Hotel.

Shaw's Creek, which flows beside the main street, attracted various mills to the water power of this swiftly flowing waterway. Two early grist mills were built, but later burned. In addition there were a pair of woolen mills. Dods Woolen mill, also known as the "upper mill," as it is about a kilometre upstream from the village centre, was built in 1880, replacing an earlier frame building. This four storey stone structure is now the popular Millcroft Inn and Restaurant. Closer to the centre of the village, and north of Queen St, William Algie built a three storey stone woolen mill, known through most its life as the Beaver Woolen Mill.

One of the most prominent and striking buildings on Queen St was the Boggs and Rowcliffe, or Barber Bros, Carriage Works. A massive two storey stone building, it stood on the south side of Queen nearly opposite the woolen mill. Built in 1892 to replace an earlier frame building, it has housed over the years a paint shop, munitions factory and a tool and die works. In the 1980s it was renovated and operated for a number of years as an antique store. Sadly and inexplicably, in the early 1990's it was demolished and replaced with a vacant lot.

Despite its early prosperity, it was the proximity of the rapidly growing community of Orangeville that relegated Alton to a commercial backwater. The railway chose Orangeville as a divisional point, and rail operations were concentrated there. With the advent of the auto age, shoppers chose the many shops on the main street of Orangeville over the few in Alton. Gradually nearly all the Queen St businesses closed, making it almost a "ghost" main street.

Your short tour will start at the southwest corner of Main and Queen where the Dixie Hotel has been converted to apartments, on the southwest corner. A more recent extension to the building is on its west end. Next door to it, the current barbershop occupies the former post office, a building of more recent vintage. Note the historic mural on the side. Then there is Ray's Bakery and the Lyndia Terre gallery, both in early commercial buildings.

Alton's mill pond sits beside the main street.

At the corner of Victoria stand two other commercial buildings, vacant at the time of writing, and likely soon to be removed.

Across Queen St from the two empty stores stands a single storey brick building that formerly housed the Mechanic's Institute and library. The vacant lot on the southwest corner of Victoria represents the "heritage" of the carriage works.

Here, too, you will find the lane that leads across the river to the lower mill, now in the process of being converted to artists' studios, including Paradox Designs and Toad Hollow. Back out on Queen St another former store stands on the south side, and a plaqued heritage structure on the north that represents the former science hall. It and its neighbour to the west are both two storey brick buildings and likely date from the 1880s.

West of this point, the commercial section of the main street gives way to its residential section and a selection of grand homes on the south side and some examples of early workers' homes on the north side. The upper mill, or Millcroft Inn, lies about a kilometre further west.

Although its early main street buildings seem destined to disappear, this "ghostly" vestige, with its small river beside it, makes for an unusual glimpse of a once-prosperous commercial core.

Directions

 Queen St runs west from its intersection with Highway 124 about 12 km south of Orangeville.

Ansnorveldt

... a taste of Holland...

The Dutch settlement of Ansnorveldt consists only of its main street. And there is a perfectly good reason for this—it sits in a marsh. Not just any marsh, but Canada's most prolific marsh, as well as its largest vegetable garden, the Holland Marsh.

Before 1925, the marsh was a dank, wooded wetland; its only economic use was the cultivation of marsh hay. But even before the First World War, a physics professor at the University of Guelph named William Day had visited the location and became convinced it could be converted into a vast vegetable growing area.

However, neither the provincial nor local governments expressed interest, suggesting instead that Day go to the private sector. Unfortunately, since instant profits didn't seem likely, the private sector turned him down, too. Then, with the war raging, other priorities prevailed. Finally, in 1923, Day moved to Bradford and began to work full-time at bringing the marsh into production. After producing a petition in support of drainage that was signed by most of the existing landowners, the municipalities sat up and took notice.

Soon, the reclamation scheme was under way. Two canals were dug along the sides of the marsh to hold the water that would have flowed into the marsh from the headwaters. A pumping station was built near Bradford and soon an area 28 km long and 6 km across resembled a vast treeless prairie.

Now all it needed was people.

One person who took note was a Dutch immigrant named John Snor. Head of the Netherlands Immigration Foundation, he was concerned about the possible deportation of Dutch immigrants who had been made jobless by the depression. In 1933 he developed a plan to relocate a number of these Dutch families to the marsh. There he assembled for their homes a 125-acre parcel of land that included a small strip of land along what would later become Dufferin Street.

Funded jointly by the federal, provincial and Dutch government (the municipal government refused to participate), the initial group of 19 families, most belonging to a Christian Reformed Church in Hamilton, began the arduous job of clearing stumps and creating a village.

A Netherland village named Ansnorveldt was created in the Holland Marsh by Dutch settlers in the 1930's.

Along the west side of Dufferin they built a row of identical Dutch-style homes. Each had a front-facing hip gable roof, so they all lined up in a neat row. They were small, with only a kitchen and living room on the ground floor and two bedrooms upstairs. Because of the ever-present danger of flooding, they were built off the ground. From both the front and back windows they looked out over a vast flat, treeless plain, one which soon would be producing onions, carrots, celery and lettuce and would be considered the breadbasket of Ontario.

The village was essentially complete by 1934, and was named in honour of its founder, John Snor; Ansnorveldt translates as "on Snor's field." The village streets were given Dutch names such as Bernhardt, Emma, Wilhelmina and Juliana.

Although no roads led to Bradford at this time, Ansnorveldt would not develop a commercial core on its main street. In addition to the look-alike homes, the village could claim only a school, two churches (Christian Reformed and a short-lived Roman Catholic mission), as well as Hadder's Holland Marsh Groceteriers, a small boomtown style building.

The following seven decades have brought changes to the marsh. Newer homes now mingle with the old Dutch cottages, and a new school and a new church have replaced the original buildings. The grocery store has closed although the building still stands. A road has been extended east to link the community with Bradford, and Dufferin Street has been paved north from Highway 9 into the village.

As you enter the marsh on Dufferin Street, you cross the south canal, bayou-like in appearance with its overhanging trees. A short distance further on, the houses line the west side of the roadway, with the dark soil close by the roadside on the east. The new church and school are on the east side about midway into the village, with a small library located down a nearby side road. At the corner of Dufferin and Emma, a plaque commemorates the foresight of John Snor and the story of the settlement.

Dufferin Street sees little other than local traffic. Yet a few kilometres to the west, the roar of six lanes of Highway 400 traffic comes from hurrying travellers who are likely unaware that a piece of Holland lines a small main street just across the lush fields of vegetables.

Despite the popular assumption, the name of the marsh, "Holland," has nothing to do with the origin of its settlers. Rather, it was a name given to the area in 1794 by Upper Canada's governor, John Graves Simcoe, to honour the then Surveyor General for Upper Canada, Samuel Holland.

Directions

Ansnorveldt lies along Dufferin St about 3 kilometres north of Highway 9 and 10 kilometres northwest of Newmarket.

 *Arden*

... in the far hills of Frontenac...

The main street of this hill country community is a true vestige of its past. Most of the structures are original and little altered. Sadly, many sit disused and deteriorating. While they remain, Arden's main street buildings are a living legacy.

Arden began as a mill town on the banks of the Salmon River. Most of the first inhabitants had been living at Buck Lake some distance to the southwest, a community that had begun as a distribution centre for mail and other goods destined for the pioneers in the area.

Travel was either by rough and tumble stage, or by scow on the river. As more settlers moved in and cleared the tall pines from the land, a grist and sawmill were established at a water power site on the river, and the Buck Lake community was abandoned in favour of the mill site. A town plan was laid out in 1865 and the town soon boasted three hotels, a like number of stores, a church and a school, as well as the mills. Laid out in a grid pattern, Arden's "downtown" consisted of two streets, Queen and Bridge.

In 1883, the Ontario and Quebec Railway laid its rails through the area but rather than locate its station in Arden, it chose a site nearly 2 kilometres west and called the location Ardendale.

The rugged nature of the countryside hampered most efforts at farming, forcing the village's economy to depend largely on the lumber industry. As a result, the village's population has, over its existence, remained steady at around 150.

In 1937, Highway 7 was opened and traffic swept by, unaware of the little mill village tucked away in the hills. In the early 1970s, the railway was abandoned, although by this time traffic was so light that its departure had little impact.

For the most part, the decline in Arden's fortunes has left it little altered. A stroll along Queen St leads past a pair of early wooden stores, one still operating, the other abandoned. At the corner of Queen and Bridge stands the stone Anglican Church. The main street then leads south down Bridge St passing the mill on the west, now a residence, and on the east a trio of abandoned stores, all substantial two or three storey structures. The first, at the corner of Church, a weedy dead-end lane, displays an unusual covering of pressed tin. A white two storey frame store, now abandoned, lies

An early view of the days when Arden's main street was busier than it is today.

between it and a red brick two storey building that was once likely the Clear Lake Hotel. In their midst lie a number of early frame homes. Beside the pond of the lower mill on County Road 15 there is a small park.

Although this main street is not particularly extensive nor grand, it represents an unusual vestige of its heyday. While the buildings may be simple in style, they represent a rare and largely intact example of what a real pioneer village once looked like. Were the right individual to come along, as happened in the case of Merrickville, Arden's heritage could be restored, and the community would become a true hidden treasure. In fact, a few entrepreneurs have already discovered the attractions of the area and have opened such businesses as a pottery and a batik shop.

Directions

Arden lies on County Road 15 about 4 kilometres south of Highway 7, and about 65 kilometres northwest of Kingston.

 *Bala*

... a summer place...

There are few main streets in Ontario that cry "cottage country" any louder than the one in the Muskoka community of Bala. With the railway tracks perched high on one side and the waters of Lake Muskoka on the other, this diminutive main street has for more than a century been "party central" for Ontario's oldest and wealthiest cottage community. But in 1867 it was the area's logging potential that first attracted settlers to the falls carrying the waters of Lake Muskoka into today's Moon River.

Thomas Burgess is credited with being Bala's first white settler, and soon mills were located by the rushing water. At the time the river was known as the Musquosh, but was later changed by a tour boat captain who thought "Moon River" sounded more musical. And the tourists weren't far behind. When the railways reached the water's edge at Gravenhurst in 1873, hotels and resorts began to appear around the pine-covered granite shoreline, grand hotels like Rossmere, Beaumaris and the Clifton House in Bala.

By the turn of the century, the shores around Bala could claim more than a half dozen such resorts. The Clifton was renamed the Windsor Hotel, while close by stood the Swastika Hotel and the Bala Falls Hotel. When the CPR arrived in 1908, it added a station by the wharf, where crowds poured in both by water and by rail.

During the 1920s the car began to replace the steam boat and the steam train, and by the late 1960s, both had stopped calling. But by then Bala was firmly established as a busy summer resort town.

Its best-known fixture was the popular dance hall known as Dunn's Pavilion. In 1942 Gerry Dunn converted an aging ice cream parlour into an auditorium where North America's leading dance bands began to fill the warm summer nights with the sounds of Chattanooga Choo Choo and Pennsylvania 6-5000. The Dorsey Brothers, Stan Kenton, Guy Lombardo, Louis Armstrong, Duke Ellington and Count Basie all dropped by to play Dunn's.

And the main street still seems to echo them. The street is fairly short and generally bereft of grand heritage buildings, but the pink rocks, the pines and waters of the lake more than make up for its brevity.

The best strategy to stroll the street is to start at the information centre in Windsor Park. There is a small parking area, and access to a lakeside walkway. The park was the site of the New Windsor Hotel, which was demolished in the 1950s. However, a little further

Many tourists arrived at Bala's main street by CPR train, a service long since discontinued, despite continued traffic congestion.

along and across the street the Bala Bay Inn still stands as it has for 90 years. It changed its name from Swastika to Bala Bay during World War II when the swastika, a traditional good luck symbol, took on a terrible new connotation.

From the inn, the old main street leads to the right while the highway that proceeds straight ahead is a more recent bypass. The clearance under the railway bridge on the old main street was too low for larger vehicles, especially buses and trucks.

Only a few places of business line the main street, including the TD Bank that occupies the former Matt's Grocery store also on the west side. On the lake side stand a hardware store and marina, and a restaurant once named for the Cotton Club restaurant in Harlem, now known as Muskoka Jo's. The Wooden Moon occupies what was Ing's Grocery, while the Balacade is located in the former butcher shop.

Behind the stores, now altered, stands the former Dunn's dance pavilion. While the original front portion of Dunn's no longer stands, the pavilion behind it still overlooks the lake and is now called the Kee to Bala. Whether the Kee or Dunn's, it continues to attract the dance hall crowd as it has for half a century, although now with more current rock groups.

Seldom are gas stations considered to have "historic" value; however, the snack bar that occupies Dunn's Station represents Gerry Dunn's original gas station.

East of the gas station the main street rises onto one of those rocky outcrops where a small shaded park on the north side of the road offers a view over the row of stores. On the crest of the outcrop, on the south side, stands the former annex for the vanished Bala Falls Hotel. It now houses an antique store and decorating service.

The street then descends the outcrop to the South Falls, where the waters of the river gush through a control dam on their way to Georgian Bay. A small park lines the falls on the north side of the road, while the lovely old wooden St Alban's Anglican church, built in 1893, overlooks it from the south side of the road.

Across the falls, the road bends under the low railway bridge to the North Falls, which roar past what is in effect a small mid-stream island, and the site of the stone Burgess Memorial Church. Built of local stone in 1926, it is one of the most picturesque buildings in one of the most picturesque settings in Muskoka.

To the east, the railway tracks mark the site of the old CPR summer station, a vital link for cottagers trying to avoid the long and congested early highways. The service was discontinued in the 1960s, although the highways remain as crowded as ever.

Here, where the old main street rejoins the highway bypass, there is more car-oriented congestion. But on the old main street there still remains that lazy, hazy summer ambience that makes it the ultimate Muskoka main street.

Directions

Bala is on Highway 169, about 25 kilometres north of Gravenhurst, or 215 kilometres north of Toronto.

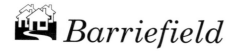 *Barriefield*

... a feel of old Yorkshire...

The first impression of Barriefield's main street is that is has been transplanted from England's Yorkshire. And that impression would not be far from the truth, for this historic Kingston area neighbourhood was largely founded and built by English expatriots transplanted from their homeland after the American revolutionary war and the War of 1812.

Following the creation of a dockyard near the mouth of Cataraqui Creek at the end of the revolutionary war, a military townsite was laid out on the hillside above it. Many of the original two-acre lots were sold by the end of 1814. A building boom occurred during the construction of the Rideau Canal in the 1820s, with the canal stonemasons responsible for many of the Kingston area's stone buildings.

Named after Commodore Robert Barrie, commissioner of the dockyard, Barriefield was home primarily to those who worked on the canal, in the dockyard or at the nearby forts. While the City of Kingston across the bay housed the upper classes, Barriefield remained solidly working class.

By the 1840s, most of the lots had been taken and growth stagnated. The railways arrived across the bay, and industries located there. Meanwhile, the military presence declined, and Barriefield has remained little altered since that time. In recent years, heritage-conscious Kingstonians have discovered the history that Barriefield represents and have restored many of the early homes. To further help the preservation effort, the City of Kingston prepared a heritage study and designated the village a heritage district, one of Ontario's first.

Among the least changed sections of old Barriefield is Main Street. While most main streets in Ontario witnessed the creation of two storey flat-roofed blocks of stores, the commercial style of Barriefield is one of separate structures with stone or frame construction and steeply sloping rooflines, much like those found in Yorkshire, England. As in many English country towns, these stores and houses closely hug the roadside.

A fitting place at which to begin a tour of the main street is at the corner of Main and James, where the two storey stone house, built in 1838, formerly housed the Pittsburgh Tavern, named after the township in which it is located.

Across the road is an imposing two and a half storey house. Built in 1814, it is one of Barriefield's oldest and was originally home to a cabinetmaker at the dockyard. Known today as Barriefield, it is the official residence of the Commandant of Fort Frontenac. Beside it and to the north is a brick residence built in 1867. On the opposite side, at the southwest corner of Main and Regent Streets, is the 1870 home built by tavern owner William Hutton.

The west side of Main St, north of Regent, presents one of Ontario's most intact early 19th century streetscapes. At the corner stands an early frame house. Beside it is the unique two and a half storey Medley combined store and house, with the preserved simple storefront on the south end, and the house entrance to the north. Next to that, hugging the road, is a string of stone structures. Built in 1834, they variously housed the Pittsburgh Inn and the Burns' Hotel and grocery. The steep rooves and massive chimneys are reminiscent of a rural Yorkshire village.

The two storey house at the end of this string was built in 1821 and boasts a pair of large chimneys and massive stone walls. Then, a short distance north of that, another two storey stone house with a wooden porch was built in 1818 as Barriefield's first hotel, the Richmond Hotel. The full second storey and the porch were added later in the century.

Meanwhile, the east side of Main Street was little developed north of Regent, with only a simple late 19th century frame house at that location.

Farther north on Main, however, is the 1843 St Mark's Anglican Church, constructed of stone and boasting a solid square Gothic style steeple. Facing the church, on the west side of the road, is the last of Main Street's early buildings, the John Marks house. For many years the church rectory, it was built prior to 1824 of log and stone and was owned for many years by John Bennett Marks, a

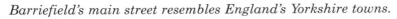

Barriefield's main street resembles England's Yorkshire towns.

prominent local Justice of the Peace and Member of Parliament.

While the main street reflects the heart of this old community, the side streets such as Wellington and Regent likewise offer images of early homes, many of them built right up to the road's edge, which again would not be out of place in Yorkshire.

Despite the sprawl that has enveloped the rural area around Kingston, Barriefield has survived as a heritage oasis, with its main street presenting a singular old world aura.

Directions

Barriefield lies on the north side of Highway 15 close to the entrance to Old Fort Henry.

 *Bayfield*

...down a shady lane...

Of all Ontario's heritage main streets, what sets Bayfield's apart are its calm shaded walkways. The many historic structures are set well back from a road that is in large part lined with mature shade trees. In many sections a boulevard separates stroller from car. And the avenue invites little through traffic. In fact, most visitors are attracted by this very feature.

Although Bayfield, like Goderich, was laid out in an octagonal street pattern, the main street, unlike that in Goderich, does not follow the octagon itself, but rather one of the radiating streets.

With no view of Lake Huron available from the street, it is hard to imagine that this village began as a vital harbour and possible fort location. The site was selected by surveyor Henry Bayfield and John Colborne not just for its possibilities as a harbour but also because the high bluff offered a view of enemy vessels approaching on Lake Huron.

The town was laid out in 1832 on lands owned by a Dutch land speculator named Baron van Tuyll van Serooskerken, Lord of Ysendoorn, or, more simply, Baron van Tuyll. The centre of the town plot was a large open square named Clan Gregor Square. A block further out from the square was the octagon. The main street, named just that, leads northwesterly from the square towards the harbour entrance, and ends not by the water but at a high bluff overlooking the lake. Now Pioneer Park, the site was the location of the village's first log building, Riley's Boarding House, now long gone.

Although the shallow harbour was less than ideal, it witnessed considerable activity with the arrival of settlers and the export of wheat, barley and lumber. But when the railways arrived, they bypassed Bayfield in favour of the deeper waters at Goderich, and Bayfield's growth stagnated. Nevertheless, by the mid-1860s it could boast three mills, four hotels, a pair of factories, four churches and several places of business. After grain shipping ended, fishing became a key business.

Although Bayfield's population plunged to less than 350 in the 1920s it never died completely. Surrounded by prosperous farms and attractive to a growing number of tourists, it has bounced back to more than 500. During the spring and fall, and especially during the summer, that number increases many-fold. One of the reasons is the main street.

The logical place to park and start is at Clan Gregor Park. Several important buildings lie around the park, including the church-like town hall on the southeast corner. It was designed to be a town hall in 1882 and was moved to this site in 1920. On the southwest side of the park the Stanbury House, built in the late 1870s, boasts a high corner tower.

The main street begins at the northwest corner of the square and extends for two and a half very strollable blocks. The first three buildings on the north side include the bank and attached residence, which date from 1867; the one time "village market," built likely in the late 1870s as a general store, a role it still plays; and the Gairdner House, built in 1855, serving variously as a store, post office and telegraph office.

On the opposite or south side of the street stands the historic Albion Hotel. The original portion closest to the square was constructed in 1842, initially as a store, but in the 1850s an addition was made to the west end and it was converted to a hotel. Both the exterior and the interior have been little altered and today it serves as a restaurant. The brick store adjacent to the hotel was built in the 1840s.

The next block of stores features, on the south side, the Village Guild, built in 1854 and converted to a gift shop in 1947. Beside it the Red Pump restaurant began life as J Whiddon's general store, but has been much altered to accommodate its new use.

Back on the north side, a few newer shops mingle with the old. The second from the corner, a two storey wooden structure, was built in 1842 and formerly housed a butcher shop. Two along from it stands what many call Bayfield's quaintest little building, today's library and archives. Although the structure is not old, dating from 1915, the arched windows are consistent with the architectural flavour of the street. The building formerly stood across the street beside the Village Guild.

The Little Inn has been restored and continues to offer fine dining.

At the end of the block stands what is probably the village's best known structure, the Little Inn. Built in 1847, it was originally known as the Commercial Hotel. Although it then sported a wrap-around porch, the present porch is part of a recent restoration. The historic old hostelry today continues to serve as an inn and fine dining restaurant.

The last of Main Street's heritage buildings is the Fowlie store, across the street and west of the Little Inn. Built in the late 1890s, it houses an ice cream shop, although many of its features are original.

Opposite the Fowlie store, today's Ritz is a 1940s replacement of an earlier Ritz lost to fire. A stroll further along leads to the residential section of the main street with such historic homes as Fairlawn, built in 1862, the Ferguson home built in 1858, and beside the Pioneer Park overlooking the lake, the Century House, which has been standing in this spot since 1841.

As early as the 1890s Bayfield began to attract summer visitors. Over the last couple of decades its reputation has spread throughout urban Ontario and Michigan, and now as you stroll the shady street, you are definitely not alone.

Directions

Bayfield is situated on Highway 21 about 20 km south of Goderich, and about 70 km west of Stratford via Highway 8 and County Roads 12 and 3.

 *Brockville*

...a bit of New England...

Ask any Brockvillian what sets their town apart from most others, and they will boast it has Canada's only New England-style courthouse square. Indeed, it is that rare configuration and the remarkable heritage buildings surrounding it that give Brockville a main street like no other.

Despite the age of the core area around King and Broad Sts, it is not Brockville's original site. That honour goes to the area around Water St where Daniel Jones built the area's first sawmill. It was William Buell who later acquired the tract of land that would become downtown Brockville.

The fledgling settlement was known at first as Buell's Bay. Then in 1808, when the government of Upper Canada moved the district's headquarters from Johnstown to Buell's Bay, the name was changed to Elizabethtown. Four years later it took its present name after the victorious 1812 war general, Isaac Brock, who was killed in battle shortly thereafter.

When Buell laid out his section of the town, he devised a New England-style courthouse square with the courthouse sitting grandly on a rise of land. From it, the vista extended down the wide avenue known as Broad St to the wharf on the river.

But the road that became Brockville's main street was King St. It followed the old wagon road along the shore of the St Lawrence River.

Despite the prominence of the courthouse, the grandest building on King St is Victoria Hall. Located at King and Market Sts, a block east of Broad St, it was built in 1862 to a design by Kingston architect Henry Horsey. It contained a concert hall, indoor market area and, eventually, the town offices.

Across the road at 2 King W the Parr Manuel Block has stood since 1845, built originally as a dry goods store.

While most of the commercial structures that line King St are relatively simple, the same cannot be said for those buildings that cluster around King and Broad Sts. The visual focus of the town centre, these places display the best that 19th century architecture could offer. At 51 King the terra cotta Dunham Block dates from 1892 and claims high arched windows. At 41 to 45 King W stands the oldest building on the main street, the Harding Building. Although the date stone reads 1904, that reflects later renovations carried out by Dr William Harding beginning in 1895. The original construction actually took place in 1832. Its simple three storey Georgian style was a common look in those early days.

Not so the elaborate Fulford Block, which looms over the intersection of King and Broad from the northwest corner. By the 1860s a drug store was operating on this corner but was incorporated into a much more extensive building in 1889. While it was William Fulford who opened the first drug store, it was his son George who gained fame and fortune by patenting a number of drugs including one promoted as being a "pink pill for pale people."

Most of the present structure was built in 1889. Its appearance reflects the more fanciful approach popular in main street architecture as the 19th century was drawing to a close. The four storeys structure was dominated by a corner tower that extended five stories and prominent gables that marked the roofline on both the east and south sides. These features have since been altered or removed altogether. Pilasters and horizontal features in the stonework give the facade a varied appearance.

Further north along Broad St, the post office and customs house was built in 1883. More Romanesque than Gothic, it was designed by a government architect named Thomas Fuller and stands three storeys high. The post office moved out in 1963 and, as of this writing, the building was for sale. On the west side of the square a row of brick homes with its collection of towers and gables marks the Publow terrace, constructed in 1895.

On the east side of the square the Molson's Bank Building predates 1853. Three storeys high and Georgian in style, its facade has been sensitively preserved and now houses the Stewart Corbitt law offices. A pair of early churches also flank the square, the 1878 First Baptist church to the east, and the 1828 Wall St United Church on the west.

Overlooking the square and the avenue, the classic style cut stone courthouse was built in 1842.

The most outstanding feature of Brockville's main street is Ontario's only New England style court house square.

But aside from the beauty of the courthouse square, the remainder of Brockville's main street could at best be described as "functional." Despite the number of early buildings, little has been done to preserve or enhance their heritage features. The three storey stone building at the southeast corner of King and Apple displays unusual third floor louvres, the Leeds County Books Building offers attractive woodwork and a dated cornice, while an interesting grouping of old stone buildings appears at the corner of King and St Paul.

On the north side of King west of Chase, a well-preserved string of three to four storey businesses still survives.

A few treasures lie off the main street, as well. The old stone mill, for example, on Water St is now a restaurant. Behind the town hall, Canada's oldest railway tunnel, built beneath the streets in 1853, is preserved in a small park. East of the town hall, King St is more residential in nature with a string of 19th century mansions known as "millionaires' row."

Hopefully, the courthouse square might someday realize its full potential with more pedestrian-oriented uses and more street life, and once again become the focus of the community that courthouse squares were historically meant to be.

Directions

Brockville lies along Highway 401 in eastern Ontario about 80 km east of Kingston and 110 km south of Ottawa.

 Burnstown

... a Madawaska main street...

Although Burnstown is barely one step above a hamlet, its humble main street typifies much of what the Ottawa Valley is all about. Here is, only slightly disturbed, the vestiges of logging days, when lumbermen used the foaming waters of the Madawaska River, which swirl by its fringes, to hurtle their logs to the massive mills in Arnprior. The buildings also relate to the time when pioneer settlers made their way into the farmlands of the Madawaska Valley by horses, by stagecoach or simply on foot.

The site was ideal for a village. The water power of the rapids on the river attracted the development of mills, while the junction of a pair of pioneer roads spawned the stopping places necessary in an era of jolting stage travel. An early description that had the valley walls rising "400 feet perpendicularly above the water" is an exaggeration, although the forested hills do rise steeply from the water's edge.

By 1863 Burnstown had become a busy mill town and an important stopping place for stagecoaches. The rapids attracted a grist mill and sawmill, while two hotels provided respite for travellers and loggers. The town could also claim three general stores, a blacksmith, wagon factory, brewery and Templars Hall. During its heyday, Burnstown gained a wide reputation for the rowdy behaviour of its loggers who were no doubt quite happy to have a brewery in town. When the post office opened in 1854, it took the name Burnstown to commemorate the Scottish poet, Robbie Burns.

Gradually the forests were cleared of their tall pines and the logging industry declined. Then when the railway bypassed Burnstown in favour of Renfrew to the north and Calabogie to the west, Burnstown became a backwater. Yet it never became a ghost town. Instead, as the Madawaska area has gained greater appeal with vacationers and those seeking country homes, Burnstown has come back to life as a small centre for artists and publishers.

Here where the Madawaska River has carved a deep and dark canyon, most of the village grew up along the north wall of the valley. A variety of wooden bridges across the river replaced one another until 1937, when the first steel bridge was built. Following construction of the Stewartsville dam in 1947, the water level rose and a higher bridge was needed. The current concrete bridge, which carries Renfrew County Road 52 north to the town of Renfrew, was completed in 1975. The high waters behind the Stewartsville dam have also covered the mill sites, although one of

Although tiny, the main street in Burnstown reflects its Madawaska Valley heritage.

Log contruction, such as on the Burnstown's general store, is common.

the millstones now sits on the front yard of a village home.

Despite its small size, Burnstown contains a remarkably intact collection of heritage buildings. The best place to start a tour is from the lookout point on the south side of the river, just beside CR 52. From this vantage point the deep canyon of the river is readily apparent, one of which was even deeper before the pond behind the dam flooded the rapids.

From today's bridge you can see the abutments of the 1937 bridge that it replaced. On the north side of the river, at the corner of CR 52 and Highway 508, Florellas Antiques occupies the 1899 school house,while across from the school, St Andrews church dates from 1889. The alignment of the original pioneer road east of this point closely followed the bank of the river and now lies underwater.

North of the current intersection is a little string of buildings including one made of logs. Now a café and gift shop, this building, which served as the general store, dates from 1854. It also houses the aptly named General Store Publishing Co. Opposite the store the post office occupies the former Good Templars Hall. Uphill from this point Leckie's Lane leads west and represents the original alignment of the river road. Today it no longer hears horses' hooves and it is now a residential side street, while Highway 508 has become the new thoroughfare. And here you will find one of the Ottawa Valley's oldest hotels, the Leckie Hotel, which went by such other names as the Anderson Tavern and the McGregor Hotel. Its largely unaltered two-storey frame construction is typical of early pioneer hotels.

While David Leckie took care of the hotel, William Leckie operated a blacksmith shop just across the road. That shop is today's Fog Run Gallery, studio to sculptor Richard Gill. A short distance to the north of Leckie's Lane lie a few more early village homes as well as Images, the studio of artist Stephen Haigh, situated in the original McLeod store.

The shops and homes of Burnstown's main street are small frame buildings, true to their pioneer roots. And that, along with its setting in the canyon of the Madawaska River, is what makes it a piece of pioneer Ontario that has managed to linger to the present.

Directions

Burnstown is about 80 km northwest of Ottawa, and 5 km west of Highway 17.

 *Chatham*

...Ontario's Inland Port...

Most travellers think of a port as being on a lake or an ocean. However, the City of Chatham, at the head of navigation on the Thames River, accessed from Lake St Clair, is Ontario's only "inland" port. The main street is tied both historically and visually to that oddity.

Governor John Graves Simcoe erected a blockhouse in 1794 to divert the Indian fur trade away from the more vulnerable Niagara and Erie locations. Later, mills began to appear along the river and as they did, shipping increased.

But the American invasion in 1813 under General Duncan McArthur destroyed nearly every mill and business as far east as the Grand River. During the 1820s and 30s settlers began to move in to take up land. Duncan McGregor built the first mill at the junction of McGregor's Creek and the Thames, and the fledgling settlement soon began to outstrip its earlier rival, Dolan's Landing, three miles downstream.

Chatham's main street, King St, derives its distinctiveness from the way it follows the bend of the historic river. The stores on the north side all back onto the waterway where early schooners and steamers once tied up. Today, in the summer, yachts, cruisers and pleasure craft, large and small, have replaced early trading vessels. Right from their moorings, modern-day captains can board a courtesy bus to stores and restaurants, a luxury unavailable to the captains of old.

The best way to fully appreciate the evolution of the street is to start in Tecumseh Park, the site of Simcoe's blockhouse, now long gone. Then cross McGregor's Creek footbridge. The original bridge stood for nearly a century before being demolished in 1992, and was replaced with the current structure. The park itself has been an open space since 1795 when it was set aside as a military reserve.

At the northeast corner of King and Fifth St stands the former New York House, a one-time grocery which imported most of its goods from New York City.

Further west, a number of early stores still stand between Fifth and Fourth Streets. Number 132 King, for example, on the southeast corner of Fifth, now the Bank of Nova Scotia, occupies a former Woolworth Store built in 1898 in what is known as the "International" style of architecture.

At the intersection of King and Fourth stands a pair of former early taverns, the former Rankin Hotel at 182 on the south side, built in 1852, and on the north side, number 181 represents the site of Claude Cartier's tavern, which originally opened for business in 1830. At one point more than ten taverns lined the river, beckoning captains and crew after what was often a treacherous sail across the tossing waters of Lake St Clair at the mouth of the Thames.

A walkway from King St across from the north end of Fourth St leads to the site of the Rankin Dock. During Chatham's sailing heyday, this was the focus of waterborn activity. Passenger vessels like the City of Chatham, the Ossifrage and the Thousand Islander would board travellers destined for such exotic locales as Detroit and Windsor. Commercial river travel continued up to the 1930s with summer outings to the resort island of Belle Island in the

Ontario's only inland port, Chatham's wharves were once crowded with steamers and schooners. Today, only pleasure craft call to visit the main street.

Detroit River. New moorings, walkways and landscaping have removed all evidence of the old wharf.

Despite the alterations both along the main street and river, Chatham's main street is one of the few in Ontario where you can stroll one way along the street and back the other way along the river. Today's scene, however, is a far cry from when steamers and schooners jostled for space in this once important "lake" port. The historic portion of Chatham's portside main street follows King from Sixth St to Third.

Directions

Chatham lies in southwestern Ontario 80 kilometres east of Windsor and about 10 kilometres north of Highway 401.

 *Cobalt*

... a heritage of silver...

Ontario has no other main street like that in Cobalt. Described by a TVO Studio 2 panel as being "Ontario's most historic town," Cobalt and its main street should not be where they are. It was only through a lucky glance at some strange rocks on the shore of Long Lake in 1903 that railway timber scouts McKinley and Darragh discovered silver. The rush was soon on, and the town of Cobalt was created on a tumble of rock ridges and dark gullies so steep that buildings had to be located wherever a small patch of flat ground could be found, and the streets were left to wind where they could.

Nearly a dozen mining headframes sprang up among the crude wooden stores and the makeshift shacks.

With the placing of the Temiskaming and Northern Ontario Railway station on the shore of the lake, Cobalt quickly grew to a population of 12,000. Rue de l'Opera, today's Lang St, was the main commercial street with stores and cafés stretching for a half mile. Silver St and Argentite St were also business streets. About the only thing Cobalt lacked was a place to buy a strong beverage. But that was soon overcome with the "blind pigs," legitimate businesses that hid booze parlours in the back.

While more than fifty mines hauled millions of ounces of silver from the ground in and around the town, most of the deposits were small and by 1930 nearly every mine had closed. Cobalt's population shrank to a mere thousand. Fires began to take a devastating toll on the old wooden buildings. Fires in 1906 and 1909 destroyed much of the town, including most of the business buildings on the south side of Lang St. Then in 1977 a carelessly tossed cigarette erupted into a conflagration that destroyed 250 of the town's oldest houses.

All that didn't leave much. Nevertheless, the buildings that still line Cobalt's main street take the visitor back to the rough and tumble days of the town's silvery heyday.

The winding main street through town is made up of Miller Ave, Cobalt St, Grandview Ave, Silver St, Prospect St, and Lang St. Its two ends are defined appropriately by old mining headframes, while various boom-time buildings are found between them.

At the west end of town the rusting Townsite #1 headframe, dating back to 1907, greets the visitor. From here, the best choice for the first portion of the route is by auto, as the road winds past a string of early stores before swinging around and onto Silver St. At this point, the railway station is an appropriate starting point as it was from here that all early visitors started.

The station itself is a large brick structure with a rounded gable above the operator's bay window. It replaced the original wooden pattern book station when the boom proved too overwhelming. The architect was John Lyle, who also helped design Toronto's acclaimed Union Station.

Back up on Silver Street, the Pan Silver headframe is an original one from the Harrison Hibbert shaft in North Cobalt, 8 km east. It was moved to this site in 1998 as an historic attraction.

On the west side of Silver St, opposite the head frame, the Classic Theatre dates from the heyday, not just of Cobalt, but of vaudeville, and was one of five theatres that brought entertainers like Herbert Beerbohm Tree and the Cherniavsky Trio to the booming town. It

A quarter century ago, many of Cobalt's main street buildings still stood behind the attractive railway station.

was restored in 1993 and again hosts live theatre.

To the south of the theatre the town hall occupies the former YMCA building, while to the north, the Miners' Museum offers a glimpse of old time-mining. Tours of an abandoned mineshaft can be arranged here.

North of the theatre, at the corner of Prospect, is the former Royal Exchange Building. It was built in 1909 and was the grandest building in town at the time. In fact, it still is. Three storeys high and designed in the classical style, its main entrance faces the corner on an angle. Its survival is due to the fireproofing installed during construction.

Behind the Exchange, later called the Fraser House, steep steps lead to the upper section of Prospect St, illustrating the difficulty of town building in such adverse terrain.

One of Ontario's most unusual buildings occupies the northwest corner of Silver and Prospect. This two storey frame building has nothing less than a mining headframe sticking out of its roof. When the Coniagas Mine closed down in 1924, an enterprising grocery store operator named Giachino purchased the shaft house around the headframe and converted it for his grocery store. What may seem to many a peculiar notion proved quite sensible. He was simply using the chilly air from the deep shaft to keep his produce cool.

Prospect then leads east to what was called the Square. A small open area, it was here that most arrivals congregated after disembarking from the train to orient themselves and find their accommodation. The row of brick businesses that line the Square today were added in the 1920s.

Standing on the south side of Prospect St, the house-like building with the pillared porch is the former Coleman Township office, and the oldest surviving structure on this street. A large brick building looming down the lane behind the old township office formerly housed the assay office.

From the Square, Argentite St leads north to the site of the now-vanished Pigtown. A neighbourhood of wooden shacks and boom town stores, it contains only one structure from those early times. The remaining area is overgrown and vacant, although the new arena occupies a portion of the site as well.

Eastward from the Square, Lang St rises up a ridge parallel to the railway tracks. Today, only the brick bank building and the ancient Hermiston miners' supply store survive on this section of the street. Beyond vacant lots, which once held more stores, stands another small cluster of early buildings. It is hard to imagine that shops such as these at one time extended for more than a half mile on both sides of the road.

A new library today stands in place of several of these. Beside it is the relocated Drummond cairn dedicated to Irish-Quebec poet William Henry Drummond, who died near Cobalt in 1907. The cairn was relocated to the library from the Drummond home, which stood south of town.

This route ends at another fitting location, the headframe for the Right of Way mine. Like that of the Townsite headframe that marks the western end of the main street, this one signals the eastern end. Located here is the still-functioning Miners Tavern, and the log black-smith shop belonging to the legendary Fred Larose. According to legend, Larose discovered a rich vein of silver by throwing his axe at a pesky fox.

From the railway bridge beside the headframe, a vista incorporates the lake, the historic tracks of the TNO now the Ontario Northland Railway and the hillsides of Cobalt where the main street winds its way.

Walking tour and driving tour brochures are available in the Miners' Museum, and offer the visitor a chance to travel the hills that surround this rocky boom town and witness the dozens of silent mines that once made Cobalt the silver capital of the world.

Directions

Cobalt lies just off Highway 11 about 140 km north of North Bay.

 Colborne

...a main street garden...

One look at the main street of Colborne is all that it takes to see that it is, indeed, unique. Not only is it one of central Ontario's oldest towns, it is also one of its more oddly shaped.

Thank the town's founder, Joseph Keeler, for that. Keeler was a Loyalist refugee who had fled the post-revolutionary persecutions in Vermont and was granted land on the shores of Lake Ontario, where the once-flourishing port of Lakeport now stands. He then invited a land surveyor named Aaron Greeley from his native country to lay out a town site.

Using a layout common in New England at the time, Greeley designed a grid of streets surrounding a village square, with an unusually wide commercial street running east from the square.

Keeler's son Joe, nicknamed "Young Joe" to distinguish him from his father, established Colborne's first store and became the town's first postmaster. He named the community Keeler's Tavern after his father's business, a building that still stands. Subsequently, to honour the tenure of Sir John Colborne as Upper Canada's lieutenant-governor from 1828 to 1836, the name was changed to Colborne.

The downtown area consists of the streets that surround the square, including King, Church, Percy and Toronto Streets, as well as King St leading east from the square. The name of the square was established as Victoria Square in 1871 to honour that era's reigning monarch. In 1907 a pair of cannons used in the Crimean War was placed in the park, and a war memorial to the unknown soldier was added in 1919.

Few of the commercial buildings, either around the square or along King St, offer much in the way of architectural or historical significance. On the east side, the Home Hardware occupies the 1874 Gordon Block, while the Gothic revival United Church dominates the northeast corner and was constructed in 1862. On the southwest corner, the town's former high school, built in 1922, has been converted into a municipal office.

On the southwest corner of King and Division St, number 3 King St West is considered to be the town's oldest house. Built in the Georgian style, the Thornton House dates from 1810. Just west of it, number 7 King W, the Regency style Cumming House was built in the 1830s and was home to Cuthbert Cumming, a retired Hudson's Bay Company trader.

On the southeast corner of King and Division, facing the square, Gulligan's Pub now occupies the former Queens Hotel, a late 1880s structure that still retains a portico. The mural on the side depicts the area in earlier times.

East of the square, King St is unusually wide. Locals claim it is a foot wider than Lindsay's main street, considered by folks there to be Ontario's widest. With the exception of the hotel, the shops that line the south side are of fairly recent vintage and uninteresting in style, but a few older, commercial blocks still stand on the north side. These include the three storey Simone Block, which has seven storefronts and was built in 1882. Further east, the two storey Coyle Block was added in 1899.

But the feature that noticeably sets this row of buildings apart is the

The landscape garden along Colborne's main street is unlike that in any other town.

landscaped boulevard separating the sidewalk from the road. A virtual rock garden, it presents a colourful arrangement of flowers and plants. No comparable boulevard has been installed on the south side of the road, nor anywhere else in Ontario.

This unusual aspect extends through to the next block, Victory Street. Here, set well back from the sidewalk, is the town's oldest church, the Old St Andrew Presbyterian Church. Construction on it was started in 1829 using stone quarried on the shores of Lake Ontario, a short distance to the south. Designed after a church in Scotland, it offers a massive square central tower and round head windows.

Opposite the church, on the northeast corner of Victory and King, stands the town's most photographed building, the diminutive registry office. This single storey red brick building is noted for its rounded windows and its barrel vaulted office. Heavy metal bars and shutters were installed to discourage theft. The building dates from 1859 and was designated a heritage structure by the town in 1996.

Between Victory and Church St a few early homes line the main street, including the 1830s Seaton House at number 57 and the 1850s Kernaghan House at number 56. The Seaton house now contains Seaton's Antiques Collectibles and Gifts.

The next street has earned its name, Church, for at this intersection stand no fewer than three churches. The oldest, the delightful Trinity Anglican Church, dates from 1846 and the rectory beside it from 1909. Tall, wooden and white, its spire is, as in many early churches, both elaborate and attractive.

On the northwest corner, the simpler Prospect Missionary Church dates from the 1850s but was used as a private residence before being converted back into a church in 1945. But the least church-like in appearance is the Roman Catholic church on the northeast corner, set amid a wide lawn. What began as the estate home of the Hon. W A Willoughby was purchased by the church and consecrated as St

This unusual catholic church on Colborne's main street was originally a private home.

Francis de Sales Roman Catholic Church. Its two storey square pattern and mansard-roofed central tower clearly mark it as residential in origin.

A short distance east of the churches is the community of East Colborne and, at the northeast corner of Parliament and King, the 1822 Keeler's Tavern, now a residence. The Keeler house itself, built in 1820, still stands a short distance along Church St east of the square. Its rare Vermont style neo-classical facade is identical to that on the much more famous Barnum House, now a museum located in Grafton.

While the commercial buildings on Colborne's main street may not date as far back as the town's homes and churches, the landscaped boulevards and the rare New England square make it one of Ontario's more unusual looking main streets.

Directions

 Colborne lies south of highway 401 about 140 kilometres east of Toronto.

 *Deloro*

..the last company town...

Deloro is a rare example of a distinctive and well-preserved "company town." Almost the whole village lines the main street.

The name "Deloro" translates as "valley of gold" and this was the reputation that it initially enjoyed. In 1866 Ontario's first rush struck the hills east of what became Deloro, where the town of Eldorado briefly boomed. Prospectors quickly flocked into the hills further afield and on the site of Deloro sank two dozen shafts. But as the gold was laced with arsenic, early extraction techniques proved impossible.

When cyanide separation was perfected towards the end of the century, operation commenced. Between 1899 and 1904 a mixture of gold and arsenic was hauled from the shafts. Then Deloro Mining and Reduction set up a silver refinery to handle silver from the newly opened Cobalt silver camps, for this silver also contained high levels of arsenic.

During World War I, cobalt was extracted from the ore containing silver and arsenic and alloyed with chromium or tungsten to manufacture stellite, an extremely hard product used in machining steel and cutting metals. The Deloro refinery became one of the few such plants in the world, and material was sent from as far away as Africa for refining.

By 1916 the workforce had increased to such a degree that the com-

The former manager's house is Deloro's grandest.

pany established a townsite for its managers and employees. Forty-five homes were built along the main street, ranging from single family dwellings to two storey duplexes. Closer to the mine were boarding houses and executive homes. A general store, hospital and school rounded off the village.

Although the demand for cobalt declined after the war and the supply dried up in the 1930s with the closing of the Cobalt silver mines, the town continued to depend upon its existing stockpile. Demand soared again with the onset of World War II, especially following the capture of the cobalt refining plant in Antwerp by the enemy.

In 1961 the company closed down its operations and buried the piles of arsenic. The houses were sold off for less than $900.

Although the population shrank to just 200, the town never became a ghost town. Today the houses all remain occupied, although the site of the mine operation and the refinery has been cleared of its structures and fenced off.

To explore this distinctive village and its main street, start at the historic plaque beside the community centre. The main north-south avenue, with the worker's homes, is O'Brien St. The short east-west street at the south end of O'Brien contains the former company store, community centre, former school, and a pair of management homes, as well as the handsome executive mansion.

From the plaque all parts of the village are easily walkable, as the employee homes extend only one and a half kilometres north on O'Brien, while the cross street is even shorter. They display three distinctive styles, all company designed, including duplexes and single homes large and small. In their midst, an anomaly is the former Central Ontario Railway station, moved here from the village of Bannockburn and altered to become a residence. It sits about midway on the east side of the street. The chief executive house is noted for its extensively landscaped lawn and the word "Deloro" outlined in whitewashed stones. It lies east of the plaque. The school is a few paces to the west.

Although the village once elected its own municipal council, that function ceased to exist with municipal amalgamation. Now the village is strictly a residential enclave. Its uniform company residential architecture makes the place a rarity in southern Ontario where, unlike the mining districts of the north, company towns were relatively rare.

That doesn't mean, however, that it is exactly unknown. Controversy has swirled during the last decade around the responsibility for the pollution of the nearby Moira River and the ground caused by the buried arsenic. As a result the refinery grounds, adjacent to the executive mansion, are strictly off-limits.

Directions

 Deloro is situated about 60 km east of Peterborough just off Highway 7.

 *Emo*

... an international view...

From the sidewalk on the main street of this little Rainy River town you could throw a stone and have it land in the United States, Minnesota in particular. While stores line the north side of the street, the south side slopes down into the Rainy River, the waterway that forms the international boundary between the two countries.

Its history, too, is peculiar to the area. When free land under the Homestead Act was opened in 1881, the only way to get to it was by steamer along the Rainy River. As a result, a number of small steamer wharves were built to allow the anxious settlers to get to their new land. In 1892, the Department of Crown Lands published a book touting the rich black soils of the area, and the influx accelerated. Steamers like the Hosca and the Agwinde ploughed across the Lake of the Woods and along the shallow waters of the Rainy River between the new CPR railway station at Rat Portage, now Kenora, and the ancient trading post of Fort Frances. By the wharves a number of steamer villages grew up. One was Emo.

In 1897, the townsite of Emo was surveyed and named for a river in Ireland. The main street was Front Street, which ran along the river opposite the steamer landing. The Canadian Northern Railway completed its tracks in 1901 and built a large two storey frame station a block north of Front Street. When it did, the steamers vanished from the waters, and the landing disappeared.

Within a few years, more than a dozen shops and businesses lined the river bank, including the Langstaff-Schurg mill, and the three storey Grand Union Hotel.

Most of these structures were frame and two storeys high, many sporting the boom town facades common in northern Ontario's early towns. As could be expected, fires took their toll on these flammable structures. The Grand Union Hotel was lost to flames by 1910, and in 1929 nearly half the street burned.

Following the fire a few were replaced with structures of concrete or brick. One unusual effort was the Nuttall Block. In 1926, a local blacksmith named Robert Nuttall single-handedly completed a two storey concrete block building. The grandest building on the street, it contained a string of six stores on the ground level, featuring semi-circular transoms and pilasters between each. The windows on the second floor looked out over a balcony. Following Nuttall's death the building was allowed to deteriorate and eventually had to be torn down, a loss that is locally lamented even today.

By 1980, only three original buildings had survived the fires and replacements, Meyers Clothing, the Langstaff Block, and the Emo Hotel. And although the store is not original, the Tomkins name has been prominent on the main street since the beginning. A few others, such as the bank, date from the 1929 fire.

Despite the changes, the overall streetscape, a line of stores facing across the river to the American side, retains its early aspect, one that no other main street in Ontario can offer.

 Emo is on Highway 11, 370 km west of Thunder Bay.

 *Formosa*

...where opposites attract...

From the wide and fertile farmlands of Bruce county the silvery steeple rises high above a grove of trees. This is nothing unusual in rural Ontario. However, as you pull in front of the church the land suddenly drops away into a wide unannounced valley in which nestles the village of Formosa. Its distinction lies not in its buildings, but in its geography. It also lies in the contrasting but equally historic structures that mark each end of the street and define its history, the large Catholic church atop the north valley wall, and the brewery on the south valley wall.

The church is the Church of the Immaculate Conception, a soaring cathedral-like house of worship built in 1883 for a community of German Catholic settlers. Designed by Joseph Connolly, it was built using local stone and restored in 1975.

A landmark in most of Ontario's early German towns was the brewery, and on the south valley wall, 2 kilometres from the church stands Formosa's other notable landmark, the Formosa Springs Brewery. In 1869, Andreas Rau moved from New Hamburg where he had operated a brewery, to Formosa, then a small sawmill village and the heart of a growing community of fellow German immigrants.

Following a series of fires and ownership changes, in 1884 the brewery fell into the hands of Francis Xavier and Anthony Messner. By this time the little industrial village had boomed to 600 residents

The main street in Formosa is tucked into a scenic valley.

with two schools, five general stores, several hotels, three blacksmith shops, two wagon shops, a grist mill, a carding mill and a cigar factory. Its population today hovers around 300.

The village's brewing heritage seemed threatened when in 1971 the company moved its operations to the outskirts of Barrie and then was sold to Molson's. The brewery had gained fame, or notoriety, by being the only one in southern Ontario to remain open during the well-remembered brewery strike of 1968. Its four brands of beer, Diamonds, Hearts, Clubs and Spades, made their way into Ontario homes in unprecedented numbers. Then in 1989, the Algonquin Brewing Co re-opened the plant and it once more has become a popular destination for beer connoisseurs.

In the parking lot of the church, a plaque recounts the history of this historical and impressive building. From here the view extends through the trees across the valley.

While most of the village's early businesses no longer survive, the Formosa Inn now occupies the former Formosa Hotel, built in 1885, while a convenience store occupies the 1866 Omer's store. Both lie at the foot of the hill below the church. Along the main street, Bruce County Road 12, which crosses through the valley, are a string of early homes, largely identical and likely those of the workers in the many factories and the brewery.

Along the main street is another unusual natural feature, randomly placed, rounded rock outcrops. Appearing as if they had been simply placed by a giant hand, they resemble huge boulders. In fact, they are erosional remnants of a porous limestone layer of bedrock that consists largely of coral. The best view of them, in addition to the main street, is in the Lion and Lioness Park at the south end of the valley. Beside this little park, a small sign commemorates the first sawmill on the site in 1850. This geological phenomenon also gave rise to the clear springs that became the brewery's claim to fame. The Palace Gardens were created around the springs as well, but are now privately owned.

After climbing part way up the southern valley wall you come to the entrance of the brewery. The house in which the outlet sits is the 1869 house built for brewmaster Rau. It has been restored by the Algonquin Brewing company and a plaque recounts the story of the industry. Then, continuing south from the valley, you are back up on the green hay fields, and the valley behind you has vanished from view as if it never existed.

Directions

Formosa lies close to Highway 9 about 85 kilometres northwest of Kitchener.

 *Galt*

...a European touch...

Many visitors to Galt's main street say it resembles a European city. Old stone buildings hugging a river, church spires stabbing the sky and preserved heritage bridges all combine to remind them of a place not unlike Florence. Although Galt is not as old as that historic Italian city, its main street and riverside heritage remain remarkably intact and noticeably "European."

Many of Ontario's earliest non-native settlers made their way up the Grand River, establishing mills and communities at the many water power sites along the way. At this location William Dickson acquired 90,000 acres of land and retained Absolom Shade to develop the site. Known initially as Shade's Mills, it developed slowly until the Canada Company's John Galt opened a road link with his headquarters town of Guelph. In appreciation the happy citizens renamed their community after Galt.

Galt then began to grow into a busy mill town with solid buildings that predate the arrival of the railways, many of them built of limestone and granite.

Main Street starts, like one in Europe might, at a town square overseen by a pair of churches. Queens Square, created when the town was first laid out in 1816 by William Dickson, lies between George St. and Grand Ave. on the south side of the Grand River.

Around the square, two heritage buildings are the Knox

This vista of Galt's main street bridge is reminiscent of a European scene.

Presbyterian built in 1869 and its neighbour across the square, Central Presbyterian, added in 1880. The presence of two churches of like denomination reflect a wide-spread rift in the Presbyterian church in 1869, which resulted in the Knox congregation splitting away and joining other congregations to form the Central church.

Closer to the bridge, on the southeast side of the square, the Hume's Block dates from 1856 and represents the oldest building around the square.

The European ambience is enhanced by the graceful bowstring bridge across the river. The first crossing was put in place in 1819 followed by a succession of wooden and iron bridges, most of which were destroyed by the river's notorious and regular floods. The present structure was erected in 1931.

Several wonderful early stone buildings line the river on the east bank. Lining Water St to the south of Main are the Commercial Building, number 11 Main, which dates from 1850. Occupied since the 1860s by the Bank of Commerce, the three storey structure is noteworthy for its stonework and its rounded corner entrance. South of Main, on the west side of Water, is the 1885 former post office. It, too, is constructed of stone and displays typical post office features such as its steeply pitched Gothic roof line and the corner tower. Today it houses the Fiddlers Green pub.

Next to it stands another equally remarkable and massive building, the Imperial Block. It was built in 1887 and contained a variety of commercial enterprises including a bank, grocery store, tailor shop, dressmaker and dentist. It is constructed of brick in the Romanesque style of architecture.

Then, immediately south of that, although less elaborate in style, is the area's oldest surviving textile mill, the former Galt Woolen Factory, built in 1843. A simple stone building, it reflects the style of construction that typified most of Galt's many early mills.

Several commercial structures between Water and Ainslie on Main date from the late 1800s. Most are stone and display a variety of architectural styles from Romanesque to Italianate to simple Georgian. The two Osborne Blocks, numbers 55-63 and 51-53, date from 1895 and 1865, respectively. The Romanesque Buchanan Block at 63-69 was built in 1894. The Italianate James Young Building at 43-49 dates from 1879, while the Wilkins Block at 30-38,with its granite construction, goes back to 1863. Another pair of early granite buildings stands at 18 and 20-22 Main, built in 1872. But Main Street's oldest structure is that located at Main and Water, on the southeast corner. Known as the Granite Block, it was built in 1851. Many of these structures have preserved their ground level facades as well.

Much of the core's European flavour is found on Water St north of Main where a landscaped walkway follows the river. The views of the bowstring bridge, the riverside stores and the church spires from this angle lend the vista a decidedly European ambience.

Known locally as the "Living Levee" the walkway was created following a disastrous flood in 1974, and was designed both to contain high water and to provide a pedestrian corridor along the river. Here is another string of early Galt buildings including the Bank of Toronto, numbers 2-4 Water St N, built in 1912, Scott's Block, another Romanesque structure dating from 1890, numbers 10-16, and the Carnegie library built in 1905. Opposite the library stands the current post office, of more recent vintage but built in a grand stone style which complements the flavour of the main street area.

A stroll north along the levee leads through the Mill Race Park, built from the ruins of the Turnbull Woolen Mill, to the stone Dickson Mill, built in 1842 and now renovated into a restaurant.

In 1987, downtown Galt was declared a heritage district. The pride and attention evident in the appearance of Galt's main street confirm that such a designation is not just warranted but joyfully celebrated as well.

Directions

The old section of Galt lies on Regional Road 24 about 7 kilometres south of Highway 401 within the City of Cambridge.

☷ *Glen Williams*

...old mills, new life...

Almost lost amid Georgetown's urban sprawl, the valley village of
Glen Williams exudes a distinctly mill town ambience, little
changed over the decades. Its winding streets and historic buildings, all nestled in the valley of the Credit River, represent an oasis
away from the urban tedium which lies literally above the hill.

Benajah Williams was one of the first to arrive in the area and, along
with his son Jacob, set about erecting the area's first mills, complet-
ing their woollen mill in 1839. Another son, Charles, started up a
sawmill and a flour mill. The prolific Williams clan also ran the
local blacksmith, tannery, cabinet shop and general store, and gave
the community its name.

The village went on to add a hotel, two churches, a pair of general
stores, a school and a "town hall," which was used largely for social
events.

While most of these early buildings still stand, the village has
grown, yet it has not lost its valley village appeal. And that makes
this main street special.

The best starting place to take in the main street is the Williams
Mill studio complex. It lies at the intersection of Prince St and Main
St on the east side of the Credit River. This collection of potters,
painters, glass blowers and jewellery makers is housed in a complex
of early mill buildings which have managed to survive floods, fires

A former general store, the Copper Kettle tavern is part of Glen Williams' historic main street.

and changing times. The yellow wooden mill represents Charles Williams 1850 sawmill, the second on the site. The stone building is the former electric power plant built in 1890 on the foundations of the Williams' grist mill.

The Williams family home, an Italianate two storey brick building, can be seen on the north side of Main Street opposite the mill complex.

Another appeal of this main street is that the key buildings are huddled close to each other. Immediately east of the glass blower, the Copper Kettle pub occupies the former Wheeler store and beside it stands the brick "town hall." Further along Prince St where the road winds steeply out of the valley are several more early homes. Near the top of the valley you will find the second of the village's schools.

At the northeast corner of Main and Prince a craft shop occupies the former store where, local legend has it, a certain Timothy Eaton clerked before starting a well-known business on his own. On the west side of Main, the bakery and tea room are located in a relatively recent building. Beside it, however, an early frame duplex has been restored to much of its original exterior appearance. Just north of it an aluminum-clad building represents Hill's Hotel built in 1848 by William Alexander.

Flanking the bridges which cross the Credit River are the village churches, St John's United and St Albans Anglican. About 1.5 km further north is the massive stone form of the former Beaumont Knitting Mill.

Despite the urban fringe creeping in from nearly all sides, this historic little clutch of early buildings provides a much needed respite from the new, the familiar and the tedious.

Directions

Glen Williams lies on Prince St just east of Mountainview Rd in the northern portion of Georgetown.

 *Goderich*

...an eight-sided "Square"...

One legend, probably exaggerated, has it that a traveller set out from a hotel on Goderich's main street and complained that the street was too long and that he had never seen so many stores with the same name. The hapless voyager was of course going around in circles, for Goderich has a main street that never ends.

Laid out in 1827 by William Tiger Dunlop and John Galt of the Canada Company, a land settlement agency, Goderich contains the only perfectly octagonal main street in North America. Streets radiate out in eight directions from each point on the octagon. This unusual plan was adopted from a 2000-year-old town plan devised by a Roman architect named Marcus Vetruvius, one that was much in vogue in Renaissance Europe.

Some historians have argued that the plan was intended for use in Guelph, for why would a radiating plan be placed by a lake? It is now more widely-accepted that Goderich's name, not its plan, was intended for Guelph.

Dunlop and Galt saw the port as being the centre of their company's land development scheme for Perth and Huron counties. However, the harbour was inclined to silt, and road travel was generally preferred in any event. In 1861 and again in 1882, a pair of railways entered town, and the emphasis on the harbour faded. The centre of the town moved from the water's edge to the "square" which soon became the main street. When Goderich was named the county seat, a court house was erected in the centre of the square.

Despite the decline of the railways, and despite the arrival of suburban malls, Goderich's main street has remained active, and in 2002 was named by a panel of experts on TVO's Studio Two as Ontario's best traditional main street.

While the square can claim no single building of exceptional architectural merit, most of the structures which surround it have preserved their 19th century features.

The court house itself is a relative newcomer. It was added in 1954 when the original building burned. With its pseudo-art deco flavour, critics have complained that it is out of place amid a collection of Victorian buildings. Rather, a good starting point for a walking tour of Goderich is at the town hall, a few paces along West St at number 57. This Romanesque stone building was designed in 1890 by architect Thomas Fuller who later on, as Dominion Architect, designed the centre block of the Parliament Buildings in Ottawa.

Opposite the town hall, numbers 44-48 West St date from 1863. This building originally functioned as the Bank of Upper Canada. Between these and the square, several early buildings have been well-preserved and today house lawyers and other professional offices.

Preservation around the square, however, has met with mixed success. In a few cases, new construction has not respected the style or the massing of the earlier buildings.

Standing at the southeast corner of South St, the Bedford Hotel dates from 1874 and is noted for its octagonal corner tower and

The domed Bedford Hotel dominates one of the eight corners of Goderich's octagonal main street.

elaborate dome. Most of the ground floor facade has been preserved, and the interior has been recently renovated. Today it houses a pub, a restaurant and rents hotel rooms.

Number 35 South St, a short distance from the Bedford Hotel, was Polly's livery stable and dates from the 1840s, although portions were added subsequently. Built of stone, it displays a rounded entrance and rounded windows. The full front gable incorporates a variety of flourishes usually not associated with such businesses.

At the corner of Kingston St, number 112 Court House Square dates from 1839, and was built at a time when "downtown" Goderich was still largely at the harbour. It has been altered over the years, and its appearance is unexceptional. Still, it is the Square's oldest building.

A few paces east on Kingston St, at number 29, stands a 19th century institution, the customary opera house. While the ground level consists of more modern places of business, the tall, slender arched windows of the third floor are typical of those used to light the high-ceilinged theatre. It dates from 1869.

Between Hamilton St and North St, the block of buildings which begin with the Royal Bank, number 158, date primarily from the 1870s. The bank in particular shows a series of gothic arches beneath the cornice, and a rounded corner entrance. Similarly, across the street at the east side of Hamilton and the Square, the three-storey Bradley Block, built on a triangular parcel, shows its rounded corner design, although its cornices are much simpler than those of its neighbour.

Finally, the block of stores between North St and Colborne represents the best preserved block of buildings on the Square. A pair of matching corner buildings, three stories high, were constructed at North and at Colborne in 1873 by fur merchant William Savage and harness maker Horace Horton, respectively. The six identical two storey businesses between them were added in 1889. The decorative cornices and arched windows are consistent along the entire block, while the ground floor facades, although modernized, at least respect the overall style of the block.

Although this completes your tour of main street, there remains much to see in Goderich. Most of its old streets, particularly between the Square and the Harbour, offer up grand old homes, well landscaped and preserved. The eight-sided jail at the corner of Victoria St and Gloucester Terrace is now a museum. An authentic-looking castle, known as the McDermott Castle, overlooks the harbour from its bluff-top location on St George's crescent. The former CPR station stands by the water on Harbour St, while the former Grand Trunk station, with its twin turrets, dominates the east end of East St.

The salt mines, discovered in 1866 during a search for oil, continue to dominate the port where lake freighters and trains still call.

With its population of 8,000 and its out-of-the-way location away from major highways, Goderich is a pleasant retreat, provided you don't end up going in circles.

Directions

 The town is at the end of Highway 8, 120 kilometres west of Kitchener.

 *Havelock*

... a southern railway town...

Motorists hurrying along Highway 7 between Peterborough and Ottawa usually notice something quite different about the town of Havelock. Unlike most of the little communities on the route— Kaladar, Norwood and Marmora—Havelock is all "railway." This feature is all the more unusual given that most of the track east of the village has been gone for nearly a quarter of a century. Yet its main street still reflects a railway heritage.

In the late 1870s, railway promoters were looking for a fast route to attract western American grain shippers. A couple of fledgling railway lines were already in place: the Canada Central led to the east and just a few years later it would form the nucleus of the CPR, while the Credit Valley Railway led to the west, linking Toronto with the U.S.-based Canada Southern Railway at a junction in St Thomas. All that remained was to tie the two together.

It was to this end that construction began on the Ontario and Quebec Railway (OQR) in 1882. The selected route would lead across the rugged terrain of central Ontario, through Peterborough, and link with the CCR at Smiths Falls. To service the locomotives and accommodate train crews, a divisional point was needed halfway between Toronto and Smiths Falls.

To avoid higher land prices in existing communities like Norwood, the OQR selected a flat area of land near a village on Norwood Road named Havelock. The first station on the site was a simple two storey wooden pattern, located where Highway 30 presently crosses the track. A pair of hotels was built there along with a clutch of railway homes. However, shortly after, when the railway added its divisional yard facilities a kilometre to the east, the station was relocated there.

Here a town site was laid out using the standard grid network of streets north of the tracks. The main street appeared along the road behind the station, with the Dineen and Armstrong Hotels, a row of cafés and boarding houses.

Despite the building of a lakeshore line in 1912, the OQR route remained in use. In fact, in 1929 the facilities were upgraded and the station was replaced. Wheat trains continued to use the town as they made their way from Port McNicoll to Montreal. Food trains anxious to hurry their cargo of fruit from California and meat from Chicago to their eastern seaboard markets called as well. Four passenger trains departed each day, two connecting with Bobcaygeon and two offering commuter service to and from Toronto.

Then, in the 1930s, Highway 7 was opened, bringing more motor vehicle traffic through town.

During this time, Havelock developed two commercial cores. One string of businesses developed behind the station, along today's Highway 7, while a second core developed along George St, a block north and several blocks west.

When the era of the steam engine ended in 1953, the CPR removed many of the old yard buildings and reduced its work force. But the following year branch lines were opened to the mines at Nephton and Blue Mountain, about 40 kilometres to the north, to haul out nepheline syenite, a mineral that is used in the manufacture of glass and ceramics. Commuter service to Toronto continued off and on until 1990, when the federal government under Brian Mulroney elim-

One of Havelock's early main street businesses is located, as are most, across from the railway yards and station.

inated half of VIA's routes, the Havelock-Toronto line included.

Finally, in the late 1990s, the station was closed and sold, and highway commercial development replaced many of the old buildings on the main street. Despite all the changes, Havelock's main street continues to offer a railway streetscape rare in southern Ontario.

To start, park near the Tourist Information Office located in a new building designed to look like a small railway station, complete with a CPR paint scheme and a bay window. A caboose sits beside it.

Behind the office the train yards extend over several sidings, usually filled with cars from the mines. The narrow strip of land between the highway and the track is now given over to parking, much of it landscaped with large blocks of pink granite.

At the eastern end of the main street, the most dominant building remains the railway station. Built of brick with steep cross gables, it hugs the road on the one side and the tracks on the other. Behind it the two hotels still stand, one now a Masonic Lodge, the other continuing its role as a tavern. Stores and former cafés are found to the west of the tavern, among them a white frame two storey structure is the relocated first station.

Although passenger service has been absent for over a decade, there is ongoing pressure to restore commuter service to Toronto, a service that the rapidly accelerating gridlock of the GTA may well make necessary. And once again, railway service may come back. Meanwhile, the main street of Havelock will continue to stand apart as a real railway street.

Directions

Havelock is on Highway 7, 35 kilometres east of Peterborough.

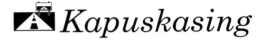 *Kapuskasing*

... going around in circles...

Not only is the main street of Kapuskasing unusual for its shape, but also for the fact that it is there at all. "Kap," as the locals refer to it, is just about as far north as you can travel by road in Ontario. In fact, when it was laid out, there were no roads to it at all.

In 1910, when railway surveyors were seeking the best route for the proposed new government railway, the National Transcontinental, they selected a location on the west side of the Kapuskasing River for a station. They gave it the name MacPherson Siding.

By the outbreak of World War I, trains had begun running, and a small main street of boom town stores grew along the dirt road behind the frame station. Because the land around it was level and stone free, the government chose the site for an experimental farm as part of its plan to encourage settlement in the Great Clay Belt of New Ontario.

Due to war hysteria, many Canadians of foreign birth were being interred as "enemy aliens". In 1915, some 1200 such prisoners were sent to MacPherson to clear land for the farm. In 1917, however, the camp was altered to accommodate real prisoners of war.

When the war ended, the government began in earnest to lure returning soldiers to the newly opened lands. Many came, but most were discouraged by the mucky soils, the severe winters and the tormenting clouds of mosquitoes and left. But it was a time, too, when

Kapuskasing's logo, long a landmark of the circle, has been replaced now by a fountain.

timber limits across northern Ontario were liberally handed out, and the Kimberley Clark Company of Wisconsin obtained a limit for the area around the falls on the Kapuskasing River. Soon after, the Spruce Falls Company was formed.

Then, in 1921, the newly-elected premier of Ontario, E.C. Drury, in an unusual initiative, stepped in and ordered the creation of a town. Anxious to encourage the development of the area, but equally anxious to avoid the pitfalls of a company-owned town, Drury was creating a government town.

But this was not going to be one of those ramshackle boom towns so common in the north. It would instead be laid out using the best planning principles and the finest architecture for the town's key buildings. The new location would be on the east side of the river and it would have a new name, Kapuskasing. Here, a new brick railway station was built, from which MacPherson Avenue led to the core of the community, its circular main street.

Although it was inspired by the octagonal main street of Goderich, this one was neither as large, nor was it an octagon. From the Circle, roads radiated in five directions, while stores were located on the outside perimeter. A small grassy area with a flagpole formed the centre of the Circle.

Approximately 15 stores and businesses crowded around the Circle. These included a couple of banks, clothing stores, a hardware store, jewellery stores, drug stores, a post office, a poolroom and the Circle Hotel. Despite the far-sighted layout of the town, far-sighted architecture did not exactly bless the buildings around the Circle. Most were the standard flat-roofed frame buildings typical of the north, with only the Imperial Bank and the post office being located in larger brick buildings.

Fires took their toll on a few of the early structures, the Circle Hotel burning to the ground in 1929, along with all the other buildings on that block.

Today, the Circle still contains a similar range of businesses. The flagpole in the centre was removed in 1971 and replaced with an attractive stylized "K" to mark the town's 50-year anniversary. In the 1980s, funds from the Ontario government's PRIDE program were put to work to further improve the streetscape of the Circle. Now a fountain stands in the centre where the logo formerly stood, and the Circle has been expanded to include benches and flower beds.

The Circle is not the only location of the town's businesses. Several are located on the streets which both radiate from and parallel the

Circle. Others are found in former satellite villages like Brunetville. More recently, a considerable amount of what today's town planners allow as "commercial strip development" has sprung up along Highway 11, which skirts the south end of the town.

Throughout the town, the legacy of the early plan is evident. Most of the residential streets are curving in nature, while the town hall, the hospital and the magnificent Kapuskasing Inn all boast chateauesque rooflines and tudoresque gables. And, while passenger trains no longer call, the fine brick station now houses a travel agency, a bus depot and a museum. An extensively landscaped park follows the shoreline of the river.

As a planned town in remote northern Ontario, at a time when even road travel was impossible, Kapuskasing is an anomaly in all senses of the word. Despite the roadside sprawl that has despoiled Highway 11 today, Kapuskasing's circular main street shows the visual benefit of good planning and foresight, even eighty years later, even in the northern Ontario bush.

Directions

Kapuskasing is on Highway 11, about 110 kilometres west of Cochrane, and 500 kilometres beyond North Bay.

 *Kirkland Lake*

... paved with gold...

Government Road in Kirkland Lake isn't called the "mile of gold" for no reason. For one, it wound its way past rocky hills that produced some of the richest gold mines Ontario would ever see. Second, it is literally paved with gold.

Following the discovery of silver in Cobalt in 1903, northern Ontario suddenly became the new Klondike, as frustrated prospectors from the Yukon tramped back east to seek the elusive gold.

With the newly-opened Temiskaming and Northern Ontario Railway paving their way, grizzled prospectors discovered gold at Larder Lake, the Porcupine and at Swastika. They climbed from the coaches at Swastika and followed the muddy winding Government Road east to the shores of Kirkland Lake.

The first to uncover glitter in the area were Bill Wright and Ed Hargreaves, and soon more gold appeared in an east-west line. By 1933, seven mines were in operation.

But the man who put Kirkland Lake on the map and into the history books was Sir Harry Oakes. In 1911, after establishing the Tough Oakes mine, Oakes looked to the waters of the lake itself where he found the richest strike yet, the fabulous Lake Shore Gold Mine.

He built a large chateau overlooking his lake. He fled to the tax-free haven in the Bahamas where eight years later he was murdered.

As the mines reaped in riches, the town grew along Government Road with a rough and tumble collection of boom town buildings. Steep rocky ridges meant stores and houses were built anywhere and everywhere. In fact, the main street had a decidedly lopsided appearance, with stores on the south side being considerably higher than the street. Paralleling the road were seven mines, stretching for over a mile, giving the town the name the Mile of Gold.

Over the years, the old ramshackle taverns, brothels and stores were replaced with newer businesses of brick. The boardwalks were ripped up and replaced with concrete. And the street, alternating between dust and mud when it was not covered in snow, would be paved. However, in their zeal to get the job done, road builders mistook a pile of gold ore for waste rock and used the priceless pile to lay the foundation for the new road. Only after the asphalt had cooled was the mistake discovered. Indeed, the main street of Kirkland Lake was now literally a "mile of gold."

Although there are few buildings of historic or architectural value on Kirkland Lake's main street, what there is tells of its golden heritage.

The extreme west end is a fitting place to start, with Harry Oakes' magnificent house. Built in 1919, it is an architectural mix of chateau and shingle styles although many believe he may have been influenced by some of Frank Lloyd Wright's prairie style buildings. It now houses the Museum of Northern History. In the chateau's parking area by the highway is the miners' memorial.

East of the chateau entrance and on the south side of the highway, the Don Lou Motel is the converted bunkhouse of Oakes' Lake Shore mine.

The main street of the golden boom town of Kirkland Lake is literally paved with gold.

Government Road leads west to Water Street, although no water can be seen. What was once the lake is now filled with mine waste, and not a drop remains. Here, on the south side of the road, number 5 marks the former site of one of Kirkland Lake's most famous brothels.

The main commercial core stores are of relatively recent vintage. The Lasalle Theatre represents the last of the town's movie houses, with its original balcony and stage.

On the south side of the street, stores and sidewalks are all built upon a steep rocky ridge and in places the sidewalk looms above the roof level of the cars parked beside it. Among them stands one of the last of the town's taverns, the Gold Range Tavern.

The buff-coloured store on the north side of the street was once a Kresge's but it also marks the former site of the home of one of the town's most colourful characters, the late Roza Brown. Ever fond of fighting city hall, Roza Brown was noted for her outspokenness and for her reluctance to bathe. She managed to become quite wealthy through her real estate dealings. In one celebrated instance, she prevented demolition of one of her condemned shacks by festooning it with paintings of the Royal Family and claiming she had signed it over to the King.

Northwest of the intersection with Duncan St, the Ministry of Mines office still provides prospectors with the information they need to continue that never-ending quest for gold. A large rock specimen at the entrance is an example of the ore that contained the golden bounty. Next door the Ontario Northland Building also displays an ore sample.

A few paces north of the main street on Duncan are the offices of the Northern Daily News, one of Ontario's longest running mining papers. A few steps further on, in the Wright Hargreaves park, are the wrought iron gates that once marked the entrance to that famous mine. They were originally located across the road to the west. A liquor store was subsequently built on top of the former mine shaft.

The head-frame of the former Toburn Mine shows how gold mining dominated Kirkland Lake's main street.

While the main concentration of commercial buildings ends around Tweedsmuir Rd, there is more to see on the Mile of Gold. At the corner of Burnside Rd stands the headframe from the original site of the Tough-Oakes mine.

The final attraction on the golden road is at Northern College. It occupies much of the Toburn mine property, where a concrete vault with a commemorative plaque is the only mine building to remain.

The back streets, too, tell of the town's mining heyday, especially along Kirkland and Kirkpatrick Streets, where early churches and boarding houses once served as places of rest and worship for the miners who once walked and worked the Mile of Gold.

.

Directions

Kirkland Lake straddles Highway 66 about 20 kilometres east of Highway 11 and 250 kilometres north of North Bay.

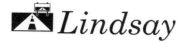 *Lindsay*

... the widest main street...

In many respects, the main street of Lindsay, namely Kent Street, is unexceptional. It runs straight for four blocks with buildings of only average architectural interest. However, if it takes longer to cross than most streets, it is because Lindsay's main street is Ontario's widest. At 100 feet from building to building, it far exceeds the more normal 66 and 86-foot widths favoured by most early surveyors.

Settlement began on the Scugog River in 1830 with the completion of a sawmill and gristmill by William Purdy and his sons. Construction of a dam raised the level of the river and allowed navigation south to the newly created Lake Scugog and the village of Port Perry.

At first the settlement clustered around the mill and took the name Purdy's Mills. The town site itself was laid out later in 1833 but the dense cedar swamp in which it was located at first discouraged settlement and by 1836 had but two residents. In fact, Kent St was not even cleared until 1840. By 1851 it had managed to struggle up to only 300 inhabitants.

Things began to change with the arrival of the Midland Railway from Port Hope in 1857, the first of several lines to converge on the town. Then with the designation of the town as the district (and later county) town, Lindsay's growth accelerated. By 1877 it had grown to 6000, an increase of 20 times in just 25 years.

Lindsay's town hall was built to include an opera hall.

Kent St, from the town hall to Lindsay St, saw the construction of two and three storey shops and no fewer than seven hotels. This section remains Lindsay's main street.

Your tour of the main street should start at Victoria Park by the armoury. The unusual width of Victoria St (which bisects Kent St here), reflects its former role as a right of way for the now vanished Victoria Railway that went from Lindsay to the town of Haliburton.

Two very theatrical structures mark the two ends of the main street: the town hall at the west end, which contained the original opera hall, and the Academy Theatre at the east end, touted as being the "oldest live theatre in Ontario."

The town hall adopted a design unusual for such government buildings, combining Italianate and classic revival themes. The windows are long and slender, topped with arches, while a two storey gable marks the entrance and a lower hip gable extension is located on the east end. A bell tower sits atop the roof. It was built in 1864. The library beside it began as a Carnegie Library in 1904 and has been considerably enlarged since.

The three storey Municipal Savings Building, one of the street's more striking buildings, stands at the northeast corner of Kent and Cambridge across from the town hall. Although the detailing around the windows and cornices remain, the decorative turrets and gables and the once-elaborate ground floor windows have either been removed or severely altered.

Of the seven hotels that once lined Kent St, three have managed to survive. The Grand Hotel, although altered, still stands on the south side of Kent St opposite the town hall.

The stores that line Kent St vary. Some have incorporated heritage themes and restored tin ceilings and transoms.

On the north side, the York Hotel covers nearly half the city block with more than twenty rows of windows. It was built as the Benson Hotel and today retains most of its historic features. Almost mirroring the hotel stylistically is the Tangney Building on the south side.

The New Royal Hotel is situated on the northwest corner of Lindsay Ave and has stood since 1861. One of Lindsay's longest standing landmarks, it has been carefully restored. Opposite the hotel on the southwest corner is number 3 Kent St, which has stood since 1863 and still retains much of its Italianate detailing.

Facing Kent St from the east side of Lindsay St is the well-known Academy Theatre. Designed by W. Blackwell, it was built in 1892 as a "modern opera house" and still functions as a summer theatre.

Directions

 Lindsay is on Highways 35 and 7, about 130 kilometres northeast of Toronto.

 *Magnetawan*

... a pioneer main street...

Despite its emergence into the 21st century, the winding main street of Magnetawan still exudes the pioneer aura that brought it into existence in the 1870s.

As the great lumber companies of Ontario moved their broad axes northward in the 1850s, they realized that the absence of a resident population deprived them of the labour, horses and food necessary to carry on logging camps. To remedy this, the Ontario government sent surveyors and road builders north from Rosseau to open a new road link with Lake Nipissing. By 1871 the Nipissing Road could accommodate winter travel, and two years later summer travel as well. To encourage settlers, the government offered the land free, provided they build a cabin and clear a few acres.

Several little villages sprouted along the route, most of them based around crude little hotels known simply as "stopping places." Once the logging companies had stripped the hills of their forest cover, the pioneers realized that the "free lands" were too rocky and infertile for farming and most headed to the newly opened Canadian prairie lands on the next available train. Farms and villages soon fell vacant.

Where the road crossed the Magnetawan River a more sizable community developed with mills and hotels and a main street of log homes and stores.

In 1886 steamers began plying the river connecting with the railway at Burke's Falls, and road traffic slowed to a trickle.

Time and fires have taken their toll on Magnetawan's early buildings, and most that remain largely serve the summer crowd and the growing number of retirees.

Still, a stroll along the main street can take the visitor back to those harsh times when the Nipissing Road was but a muddy trail through the forest and when the crude little village was a welcome respite.The placement of heritage plaques in front of several buildings or building sites helps those times come to life.

The most logical place to begin is in the small parking lot beside the historic "Nipissing Road" marker at the bridge. This location was the site of the old jail, which at twenty feet square contained four cells used mainly to house over-exuberant loggers. Beside it stood Snuggs store. Both have long since gone. On the east side of the bridge, the steamer wharf once saw frequent steamers like the Ada and the Pioneer arrive and depart from the railway station in Burke's Falls. The former wharf house, built in 1879, burned down in 2001.

South of the bridge the main street was mainly residential. Here, high on a rock outcrop, stands St George the Martyr Anglican Church, built in 1880. With its slender steeple and its rugged site, it was the subject of a 1933 painting by A. J. Casson entitled "The Anglican Church in Magnetawan."

The southern limit of the village's main street is marked by the white wooden Knox Presbyterian Church, built in 1879.

North of the bridge the commercial core of the village is still very evident. On the west side overlooking the river is the Old Country

The old church, once the subject of a Casson painting, dominates Magnetawan's main street.

Antique Shop, formerly known as the Grandview Hotel. A few paces north is the Magnetawan Inn and Restaurant. The Downtown Store, with the smaller green one-time shop beside it, dates from 1908 and has for most of its life remained a general store.

From the main intersection, Highway 520 leads east to Burke's Falls and north to Highway 124, the main route between Sundridge and Parry Sound.

While most of the early businesses that clustered about the cross-road have long gone, the Schmeler Hotel bar and restaurant still caters to villagers and visitors as it and its predecessor, the Klondyke Hotel, have done since 1886.

Directions

Magnetawan lies on Highway 124, 22 kilometres west of Highway 11 at Sundridge, and 55 kilometres east of Highway 69 at Parry Sound.

 *Maitland*

...a St Lawrence River treasure...

While Maitland's main street may not be long, it does offer a stunning collection of early 19th century Loyalist stores and houses, many of which have stood since the earliest days of travel on the St Lawrence River that flows beside it, and the ancient river road that passes through it.

The tall stone buildings that hug the roadside represent an image that has been long lost in most of Ontario's main streets. The fact that convenience stores, gas stations and fast food outlets have passed it by has helped to preserve that legacy.

Even as early as 1756, Point au Baril, as it was then called, was used for stopovers by river travellers. In 1758, a shipbuilding operation and rough fortification were installed nearby. But it was not until the 1780s that any sort of permanent settlement appeared on the riverbank.

One of the early town dwellers was George Longely, who in 1828 built a wind-powered gristmill. The windmill's stone tower soared 80 feet (25 metres) into the air, while the mill stood three storeys high and stretched 140 feet (45 metres) along the road. But the mill did not last long. With the improvement to the canals on the St Lawrence, shipping became easier and the mill closed within three decades. By the end of the century, only the tower and a few stone walls still stood. But Longely also added a store and a large stone house called Maplehurst, and these have survived to the present.

In the 1850s, road improvements were ordered, and on November 19, 1855, Maitland saw its first steam train as the Grand Trunk opened its line between Brockville and Montreal. Other industries were soon attracted to the growing village, including Charles Lemon's foundry and Robert Howieson's distillery.

While Maitland's main street added several shops and taverns, fewer than half the village lots were sold and by the end of the century Maitland's growth had stagnated. Although traffic on the river road increased with the arrival of the auto age, new homes and shopping malls were attracted to Prescott and Brockville, and, happily, Maitland remained a backwater, a fate that has preserved its early main street heritage.

The most fitting place to start a tour of the village is with the Longley complex at the west end. Maplehurst, the magnificent family mansion, still stands, set back from the north side of the road. Low-lying at a storey and a half, it was built in 1828 and is noted for its Greek portico entrance. Longley's son, George, added a home of his own in 1861 and it stands south of the road opposite Maplehurst.

The village's most prominent spectacle, however, lies just east of this house—the ruin of the windmill tower. Located immediately east of the tower, the Longely store is a two storey Georgian style structure constructed of stone and now heavily covered in ivy.

Opposite the store, on the north side of the road, a series of four houses date from the 1860s, for the most part only little altered since their construction.

The most striking string of heritage shops lies on the south side of the road, grouped around Church St, which was the pioneer road to Merrickville. The small parking lot contains a historic plaque that outlines the founding of Maitland and marks the site of an early home destroyed by fire. Beside the lot stand, in order, the Drumbville general store dating from the 1850s, the David Jones Inn, erected in 1821, and Maitland's oldest surviving building, the Levi Davis Inn, built in 1829 and missing one of its wings.

Next to these are the heavily altered 1823 Lemon blacksmith shop and the 1825 Thomas Stone house and store, both remarkably well-preserved. East of these two stone structures stands another pair of early homes, the Sheppard house built in 1825, and the Samuel Thomas "saltbox" style house, likewise built around 1825.

One of Ontario;s more unusual main street features is the ruin of Maitland's windmill.

Seldom has a main street retained such an intact collection of some of Ontario's earliest homes and businesses.

Directions

Maitland lies along County Road 2, 10 kilometres east of Brockville.

 *Merrickville*

...cafés on the canal...

With its line of ancient stores and homes, the historic Rideau Canal blockhouse, and Roman-like mill ruins, the main street of Merrickville exhibits a tranquil old-world atmosphere that no other Ontario village can replicate.

Being one of eastern Ontario's oldest communities has helped enhance that ambience. Its origins date to William Merrick, who in 1791 built a sawmill and gristmill to supply material for the pioneers then pouring into the area.

With the War of 1812 raging, the British government looked to the Rideau River as a safe alternative to the more exposed international St Lawrence River and commissioned Colonel John By to turn it into a canal.

In 1832 the canal was opened, and steamers began plying between Montreal and Kingston. Merrickville's first main street lined the side of the new canal. A new road was opened linking Merrickville with Maitland on the St Lawrence and St Lawrence Road became the main focus of Merrickville's commercial growth.

In the 1860s, mill factories and foundries augmented Merrickville's industrial base while the arrival of the Ontario and Quebec Railway (later the CPR) gave it a vital new link to industrial Canada. For an all-too-brief period, Merrickville would boast no fewer than 60 industries. However, as the 20th century progressed, new highways

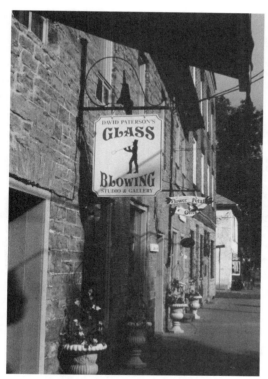

Merrickville's main street shops have been discovered by the Ottawa area's daytrippers.

and industries passed Merrickville by. Gradually its industries closed until today there is but one.

But because of the economic stagnation, Merrickville's streetscapes were spared the fast food chains, parking lots and new bank buildings that have taken a needless toll on most of Ontario's historic main streets. As recreational boating and day tripping increased along the historic canal, more and more visitors discovered the historic appeal of this forgotten little town.

Today many of the old stores now house cafés, craft shops and artists' studios. Parks Canada assumed operation of the waterway, preserving both its structures and its traditional operating techniques. Meanwhile, 33 buildings were designated as heritage structures.

The focus of Merrickville's main street is clearly the canal and its unusual military blockhouse. Erected in 1832 the blockhouse never saw combat, and is now a museum. On the north side of the canal are the now stabilized ruins of Merrick's old stone woolen mill. Built in 1848, it was considered to be Ontario's first such mill, and

The spectac-ular Jakes Block domi-nates the main street of historic Merrickville on the Rideau Canal.

is now managed by Parks Canada as an historic complex.

Here, at St Lawrence and Main, is one of eastern Ontario's most photographed buildings, the unusual Jake's Block. In 1861, Eleazar Whitmarsh built a commercial block of six stores in a building three storeys high. Built of stone, the building has a rounded corner and twelve arched windows and doors.

Just ten years after its completion, Sam Jakes, owner of the Jakes Inn along Main St, bought the building and operated it as a department store, reputedly the largest between Montreal and Chicago at the time. After a brief period of neglect between the mid-1960s and 70s, it was bought by Gary Clark and now houses the Balduchin Inn and Restaurant, a popular venue for conferences and banquets. The restoration of this building is often credited with being the catalyst that revitalized Merrickville's main street.

The preservation or restoration of most of the original stores has further helped make it unusual among Ontario main streets.

Opposite the Jakes Block stands the three-storey stone Aaron Merrick Building. Further south on the west side, at Wellington, the former Charles Holden general store, a two-storeyed stucco building, dates from the late 1840s.

On the east side of St Lawrence, the Goose and Gridiron occupies an old hotel. Built in 1856, it started out as the City Hotel, but it was more popularly known by locals as the Grenville Hotel. Today it has been renovated into an English-style pub and has been largely spared exterior alteration.

While exploring Merrickville, the other "Main Street" should not be ignored. West of the blockhouse lies an old wooden canal side depot and the former town hall, a two-and-a-half storey stone building beyond that. East of the blockhouse, Main Street contains the former school and Sam Jakes Inn. North of the canal lie more Merrick properties, including the 1821 second and third William Merrick houses, and the Merrick Tavern.

Ironically, the urban and commercial sprawl encouraged by most Ontario towns and villages has, by avoiding Merrickville, turned it into an historic oasis, with its main street a destination for those anxious to escape such icons of progress and urbanization.

Directions

Merrickville is situated on Highway 43 about 60 kilometres south of Ottawa.

 *Midland*

....an outdoor gallery...

Midland's main street, King St, is not just another pretty street. What sets it apart is its remarkable collection of outdoor murals.

Following the discovery by the townsfolk of Chemainus, British Columbia, that good quality outdoor murals can reverse a town's sagging economy, more than a dozen Ontario communities have followed suit. Places as far apart as Pembroke, St Thomas, Welland and even the much-maligned Scarborough have painted up the sides of their buildings, with mixed success.

The main street murals of Midland, however, top the list in Ontario. Midland possesses the most and nearly all were the work of a single professional artist, Fred Lenz. Born in Germany in 1931, Lenz migrated to Canada in 1951 and became known for his commercial art.

In 1991, he was commissioned by the Town of Midland, to create more than two dozen outdoor murals. His creations have made Midland the mural capital of Ontario, and the main street is the place to see them.

Historically, Midland is a relative latecomer. At a time when Toronto had already been a city for six years, in 1840 the Midland area was just welcoming its first pioneer settlers. Another thirty years would pass before the H H Cook Company built its lumber mill and a town site was laid out. When the trains began arriving, so did the industries. The Chew Brothers added their mill in 1875, grain elevators were built in 1881 and thirty years later Midland would become one of Ontario's leading shipbuilders.

Then, throughout the 1950s and 60s, the industries began to leave. The shipyards closed in 1954, followed by some of the elevators. In the 1980s the railway lifted its rails, and the station was demolished. Tourism seemed the only way to help regenerate the town's economy. Today, the main street hums with activity, especially during the summer, and motor coaches pull up to docks for the Georgian Bay boat tours. And everyone is looking at the murals.

The best place to begin this main street tour is at the library at King and Elizabeth St, housed in the former post office building, one of main street's few heritage buildings.

On the east side of King, the former Roxy Theatre, with its 1925 art deco facade still intact, has been designated another heritage structure, and it is here that the parade of murals begins.

On the side of the theatre, one of Lenz's first works depicts the area's most famous attraction, Saint-Marie-Among-the-Hurons. On the south side of Elizabeth, the Girl Guide movement in Canada is celebrated with an image of two young girls tending to an injured puppy.

A string of five murals decorates the east side of King between Elizabeth and Hugel, including three painted on the second floor of the facades at 317, 315 and 311 King depicting, respectively, Wye Marsh, the first Benjamin Moore paint ad, and Midland's 19th century harbour. All were done by Lenz in 1995.

At the corner of Hugel St, on the side of number 277 King, are Midland's two original murals, the Playfair Mill, which Dan

The only trains seen today are those on this mural depicting the town's first station.

Sawatsky painted in 1990, and beside it a view of a famous early schooner, the H.M. Schooner Bee, which he added the following year.

Facing the Sawatsky murals from the south corner of Hugel, James Playfair, the father of Midland's shipyards, is portrayed along with old photographs of some of his fleet. The corner of Hugel and King, as it appeared in the 19th century, is depicted by Lenz on the CIBC building at 274 King.

Only two murals appear on the next block of stores. These appear on the west side above 266 and 264 King. On the former, trumpeter swans take flight in the Wye Marsh, while on the latter, fittingly above the IDA drugstore, scenes from the original King St Apothecary are depicted. These are done in five panels set between textured pilasters.

Dominion Ave harbours the next set of murals. On the northeast corner of Dominion, along the side of number 239 King, a steam train is shown arriving at the original Midland station. Covering the entire length of the building, the mural consists of three panels set between the building's brick pilasters.

A short distance west along Dominion, along a laneway on the north side of the street, a painting of the harbour and grain elevators, based on a 1910 photograph, is on the back of number 236 King; facing it from across the lane is an old livery stable showing Midland's first car.

On the south side of Dominion, again in the laneway, are an early view of the harbour and an enlarged depiction of Midland's 125th anniversary commemorative postage stamp.

Atop number 235 King, a seamstress is shown by her window overlooking this very section of street as it appeared a century ago.

Between Dominion and Bay, the second floor of the Rona Dining Room depicts an early sawmill, while on the side of number 226 is a 50-foot by 28-foot (15 metres by 9 metres) mural of the historic Breboeuf lighthouse. One of the few not done by Fred Lenz, it is the work of a trio of artists named Adamson, Hauley and Templeton and it was done in 1999. The ground level facade of numbers 205-207 King shows the interior views of the general store that stood on this site in 1895. The present building dates from the 1950s. And finally, on the side of number 212, and right in front of the Chamber of Commerce building, is Lenz's 1998 view of French Canadian coureurs de bois gazing over the Thirty Thousand Islands of Georgian Bay.

While the main street ends here at Bayshore, the murals do not. On the waterfront the dock master's building boasts a pair of Lenz's

Many of Midland's main street stores have murals above the ground level.

smaller murals, one showing cruise ships of the 1890s and the other a harbour scene from the 1920s.

But the granddaddy of the murals faces the main street from across the harbour. There, on the far side of the harbour, covering the entire side of the Ogilvy grain silos, Lenz's massive mural portrays a pivotal point in the area's early history, the meeting of a Jesuit priest with a Huron Indian. It was while working on this masterpiece in 2001 that Fred Lenz died. The giant mural was finished by his sons Robert and Stephen and a family friend, Michele Van Maurik.

The murals of Midland stand apart from many other similar initiatives as most of them represent the art of one particular leading Canadian artist, are beautiful in their execution, imaginative in their placing, and are carefully maintained.

Directions

The murals of Midland are considered to be Ontario's best and make this main street unique. Midland lies on Georgian Bay about 150 kilometres north of Toronto.

 *Millbrook*

... a diamond in the rough...

Millbrook is one of those places few seem to know about. It lies well off the beaten path of major highways and rail lines. Yet, tucked into the valley of Baxter Creek, in the rolling hills southwest of Peterborough, Millbrook's main street is something of a hidden treasure.

The community began early when John Deyell built a mill on Baxter Creek in 1816, and the mill site became the commercial focus for the growing farm population. But it took the arrival of the Midland Railway in the 1850s to fuel a boom in growth.

Because of the steep valley walls, the Midland Railway was forced to lay its tracks above the valley a kilometre west of the creek. Here the railway established a key junction, with the main line from Port Hope extending northwest to Beaverton and ultimately to Midland, and a branch line curving northeast to Peterborough. While the main street in the valley flourished, a smaller commercial core developed around the station.

At its peak Millbrook could claim three hotels, two mills, a main street of two and three storey stores, and Canada's first mounted military band. The boom collapsed in the late 1800s when the CPR opened the Canadian West to wheat farmers, and it is estimated that more than half of Millbrook's population of 1500 followed the cry and headed west, too.

Eventually the line was lifted and the station removed. While new highways were built along the lakeshore to the south and later to Peterborough and Lindsay to the north, Millbrook remained a backwater. This, however, has meant that many of the buildings from Millbrook's heyday have survived.

Because so many of Millbrook's visitors would have arrived at the station, that is an appropriate place to begin a tour. While the station has long gone, replaced now by housing on the south side of King St, the small commercial core it spawned still survives. In addition to a pair of former stores on the south side of the road, the most notable building is the one-time station hotel on the north. The unusual five-sided shape of the building reflects the original orientation of the tracks.

Between this mini-commercial core, and the main downtown, the main street passes a string of elegant old homes and churches, most of them built shortly after the arrival of the railway in the late 1850s.

The core area of the main street begins as the road descends the steep valley wall just east of Collins Lane. Number 14 King St West is a large Italianate house built for the Millbrook Banking Company. It dates from 1880. Beside it stands the Richard Howden house, built in 1876 for the village's first reeve. It was designed in a Gothic style that is especially evident around the windows. In turn, beside the Howden house, number 8 King West is a more fanciful style home built in the 1880s, and it reflects the more adventurous architectural styles of that period.

Next comes the former Waverley Inn, a three storey brick building with decorative windows and a well-preserved facade. Dating from 1878, it has served as a boarding house, a hotel and a restaurant. Today it is an apartment building.

At the northwest corner of King and Union Streets, the post office is of noticeably more recent vintage, having been added in 1939 and using the art deco style fashionable in the 1930s.

The southeast corner of this intersection contains two of the village's more interesting structures. Facing King St is the former Cavan Township Hall. Dating from the 1880s, it boasts a slender cupola, arched second floor windows, two storey pilasters or false columns that extend all around and a portico entrance with balcony above it. Behind the hall and facing Hay St stands the 1881 Italianate style fire hall. Made of brick and claiming a five storey tower, it remained in use until the late 1960s and now houses a museum that includes a 19th century hand operated pumper.

The store area of the village stretches for a short block east of the hall to Tupper Street. Overhead wires have been removed and decorative street lighting and benches have been added. Many of the storefronts have incorporated heritage signage. A couple of the more outstanding stores include the Bulk Foods store with its multi-coloured bricks and the Robert Harding Building on the south side. The Wood and Kells Building at number 17, a former dry goods store, is one of the more prominent commercial buildings with its mansard roof, tower and pilasters.

Early photos of the main street show that the north side was lined with two and three storey buildings of Italianate design. Unfortunately, most were destroyed in a fire in 1876 that levelled the entire north side of the street.

A short stroll down Mill Street leads, not surprisingly, to the old mill. Smaller than the original, the Needler Mill that stands today was built in 1909 to replace the larger mill destroyed by fire in that year. It has been restored and preserved.

Millbrook's former hotel is now an apartment building.

East of the main part of the village, and up the east valley wall, the castle-like homes of Robert Deyall, son of the village's founder, and Alexander Armstrong look out over the valley. Here also is the large village school, the Dufferin School, built in 1889, preserved and serving as a community hall.

It is surprising what unusual heritage treasures await the visitor when venturing off the beaten path. And here in the valley of Baxter Creek, the little main street of Millbrook is one of them.

Directions

Millbrook lies on County Road 10 about 20 kilometres southwest of Peterborough.

 *Moosonee*

...a frontier main street...

Located on Ontario's Arctic fringe, not only is Moosonee's main street distinctive in its appearance, but it is also the last of its kind. It is Ontario's only surviving frontier main street. Although the street is wide and dusty, the boardwalks have been replaced with brick sidewalks, and the muddy main street has been roughly asphalted.

Like most frontier towns, Moosonee is not all that old. The first buildings on the site were a Revillion Frères trading post, constructed overlooking the Moose River in 1904. Across the wide waterway, Moose Factory, by contrast, holds Ontario's oldest buildings, part of the first Hudson's Bay Company trading post established in the 1670s.

Moosonee remained little more than a trading post and Cree village until 1932, when the Ontario Government pushed the rails of the Temiskaming and Northern Ontario Railway into town, in the overly optimistic assumption that this tidewater location would develop into an ocean port. The shallow shifting sands of the river made the harbour unnavigable for all but small barges and Cree freighter canoes.

However, with rail access it became the jumping-off point for the many Cree communities scattered further up the James Bay Coast. By summer, supplies would be barged to these villages, and by winter they would be hauled through the woods by tractor trains. It became and remains Ontario's Arctic frontier town.

Although there is now air service, rail remains the most popular way to arrive either by the popular summer tourist train, the Polar Bear Express or the year-round mixed Little Bear train. The main street stretches from the wooden train station for about a kilometre to the river.

Frontier towns tended to eschew fine architecture, preferring instead whatever kind of building was quick to build and most practical for its purpose. Nevertheless, there are a small number of newer buildings with architectural merit to them. The station, for example, although small and practical, has fine proportions and is one of the more photogenic buildings in town. A few railway workers' cabins huddle close to the tracks.

The nearest features to the station are a chip wagon and a train coach, the latter

Showing a Cree interpretation of the Bible, this stained glass window is one of twenty installed in Christ the King Cathedral.

converted to a museum that opens on occasion. Both let you know that you are in Cree country, for the signs are in both English and Cree.

The next buildings include the new school and the police station, and, on the north side of the road, built to resemble a stylized teepee, is the James Bay Education Centre, or Northern College. The foyer, when open, contains a display of Cree crafts and canoe building.

On the south side, and open afternoons during the summer tourist season, is the Roman Catholic Christ the King Cathedral. Although typically beautiful on the outside, the real treasures lie inside. These are the remarkable series of twenty stained glass windows designed by the native artist, Keena. They depict religious and native scenes, but from the Cree perspective.

On the north side of the street is the busiest building in town, the Northern Store. It supplies most of the community's needs with groceries, clothes, books and music; it also doubles as the local liquor store. Most of the buildings along this portion of the street are functional to the point of being frankly unattractive and include a mini-mall on the south side and a bank on the north. Beside the bank are the only buildings to date from the arrival of the railway when most of the street had a wooden boomtown appearance.

The Sky Ranch Restaurant, also on the north side, may have little appeal from the outside, but inside there is a popular local café. One building with imaginative flair is the Arctic Arts building located near the river. The log, fort-like structure contains a café, craft shop and a bed and breakfast. The U shape of the layout encloses a small courtyard.

Although the main street ends at the river, Revillion Road, which hugs the riverbank, offers a few more attractions. Here you will find the docks for buzzing freighter canoes, one of the more popular attractions for tourists. Extended canoe-shaped motorboats, these fast and maneuverable little craft constantly ferry local residents, tourists and freight back and forth across the river, primarily to Moose Factory Island. Moose Factory has a greater population than Moosonee, the former with about 3500 inhabitants and Moosonee home to about 2000.

The two main lodges are also located here, the Polar Bear Lodge and the Moosonee Lodge, which was closed as of this writing. Beside them, the old Anglican Church operates a basement café offering tourists light snacks and locally made crafts. A few paces north of the church stands Moosonee's only true historic building, the last of the Revillion Fréres trading post buildings. With its clapboard siding and its mansard roof, it has stood here since 1904.

Much newer is the Ministry of Natural Resources building a few more paces north, a vital function in this part of Ontario. The foyer offers excellent displays of local wildlife and geology, as well as a selection of videos of local significance. On the riverside is the Two Bay Tours excursion office, where tickets are available for the launch to Moose Factory or to other destinations such as Fossil Island and the open waters of James Bay, some 20 kilometres away.

In function and appearance, the main street of Moosonee fulfills the image of a "frontier" main street, and it is Ontario's last.

Directions

 Moosonee lies near the coast of James Bay about 260 kilometers noth of Cochrane and is accessible only by train or air.

 *Neustadt*

...it's because of the beer...

Sometimes it takes only a single outstanding building to turn an otherwise ordinary main street into something special. In the case of Neustadt, in midwestern Ontario's German heartland, it's that finest of German traditions, the brewery. One of Ontario's most-photographed small town structures, the 1859 Neustadt Spring Brewery is made of local fieldstone, and marks the southern entrance to Neustadt's main street. It is also one of the town's oldest buildings and dates to the earliest days of settlement in the area.

One of the last areas to open up to settlers in southern Ontario was the vast watershed of the Saugeen River. Known as the "Queens Bush," this forested region of ridges and swamps covered most of what is today southern Grey and Bruce Counties. In 1839, when southern Ontario had largely been settled, Charles Rankin surveyed the Sydenham Road from Fergus to today's Owen Sound, then called Sydenham. As farm lots came onto the market, many of the Germans who had settled in the Waterloo area moved north.

One of the first to occupy what became Neustadt was David Winkler, who bought 400 acres of land around Meux Creek, a part of the south branch of the Saugeen River. Here he erected a dam and sawmill, and laid out a town site, naming many of the side streets after his children. Shortly afterwards, John Weinert added a tannery, and finally, in 1859, Henry Huether arrived and built a fine stone brewery, a popular fixture in most of the area's German towns and villages.

By 1865, the Smith Gazetteer would describe Neustadt as a "thriving village" with a population of 300 whose industries included a flour mill, sawmill, three stores, three hotels, and, of course, the brewery. By 1880 it had reached 800 and had added a cheese factory, a furniture factory and a German language newspaper, the *National Zeitung*.

Over the last century, the population has remained much the same. So have many of the town's buildings from that era, as a stroll down the main street will reveal.

The natural place to start is at the brewery on Jacob St. Completed in 1859 just as the village was starting to boom, it was known originally as the Crystal Spring Brewery. Two storeys high, the fieldstone building stretches along the road and is attractively situated on a slight rise of land as the road curves into the centre of town. A hotel was attached to the north end of the structure. Beer was brewed in copper kettles and aged for six weeks in oak barrels, after which the kegs were sold throughout the Grey and Bruce county area.

In 1916, prohibition in Ontario closed many of the province's breweries, and the old stone building was put to use variously as a creamery, an egg grading station, and even as a town hall. In 1975 it was designated as a heritage structure, and today functions again as a brewery. Now more tourist-oriented, it sells its product on the premises, which also contain a small gift shop.

Indeed, day trippers have discovered Neustadt. Richard Mund's Pottery is found in an early house near the brewery and opposite the 1869 St Peters Lutheran Church, while opposite the brewery is the Mill Creek Woodworks. Where Jacob St merges with Mill St, the feed mill on the west side now houses an antique market. Here the village offices were located in the former fire hall, while on the east

The Neustadt brewery

side of the street, at the northeast corner of William, the former Kalbfleisch store is now a private residence.

From this intersection, Mill Street leads north. Here many early shops and stores have found new uses. On the east side, a groceteria occupies a former general store and opposite, Village Imports occupies the original 1898 Derbecker Store. On the northeast corner of Stephania is another of the town's more historic buildings, the stone Commercial Hotel. Now a private home, it was also one of the village's first hotels and dates from 1862.

A few paces north of the old hotel on the east side, another stone building, also dating from Neustadt's formative years, has housed a shoe store, a grocery store, a craft store and a library.

The main street ends at Queen St where, on the southeast corner, Granny's Store now occupies the later Derbecker Store. The store beside it is the former Weber hardware store. Now catering to day trippers, Granny's specializes in quilts, fabrics and notions. It is an attractive two storey brick structure with an upper floor balcony.

On the southwest side of this intersection is a string of attractive yellow brick stores, which once housed Hammer's hardware store. Today it contains a café known as the Country Kitchen Restaurant.

Other points of interest in the town include the modest brick house on the west side of Barbara St, a building that was the birthplace of the legendary Prime Minister of Canada, John George Diefenbaker. It is now a museum maintained by the Monarchist League of Canada.

Even without the magnificent old brewery to highlight the main street, Neustadt is a pleasant village in which to stroll, enjoy the shady streets, and simply flee from the overwhelming urban congestion that continues to creep across Ontario.

Directions

 Neustadt is situated on Grey County Road 10 about 75 kilometres northwest of Kitchener.

 *Norham*

...a vanished main street...

Tucked away in the hills of Percy Township, in the area known as the Great Pine Ridge, two villages competed for supremacy. They were known simply as Upper Percy and Lower Percy. For a time, Lower Percy had the upper hand. To relieve the inevitable confusion in names, Major Israel Humphrey, an early settler, renamed Upper Percy as Warkworth and Lower Percy as Norham, both after country villages in his native England.

Norham began as a mill site on the Percy Road, a route that originated in Colborne on Lake Ontario. For several years, Norham exceeded Warkworth in size and could boast three hotels, a liquor store, a blacksmith shop, mills, a school, a cheese factory and a church.

Gradually Warkworth, only 2 kilometres away, took over and Norham declined. In fact, it declined so far that its main street basically no longer esixts. Yet, vestiges of the village's former size are everywhere. First, there is the overall layout of the village. In anticipation of its continued prosperity, an extensive town plan was surveyed—more than 100 lots on a dozen streets. By the time Norham began to decline in the 1880s, only a few of the lots had buildings on them. Today, the scattered nature of the buildings, the empty lots that line the network of streets, and the old sidewalks taken over by weeds testify to Norham's faded prosperity.

What was the main street is today Platt Road and is paved into

Only a few scattered buildings line what was formerly a busy main street in Norham.

Warkworth. But at the south end of the main street, near the corner of Gravel Road, an overgrown gully harbours the vague ruins of the former mill. Built in 1861 by Robert Cowie, the three-storey gristmill operated until 1980. Then, in 1993, after years of standing vacant, the vandalized mill was burned down.

West of the intersection with Platt Rd, the former school stands to the south side of Gravel Road and is now converted to a home. At the southwest corner of Gravel Road and Platt Rd, a one-time store stands, also now a home.

Old village lots that line Platt Road are now mostly weedy and vacant. Another former store occupies the northwest corner of Platt and Division, while the impressive brick house at the southeast corner served as an early hotel.

In recent years, Edwards Market operated out of an addition to the north end of the hotel, but that business was closed at the time of this writing. West on Division St a few more early homes, and some more recent additions, are scattered among the old village lots.

North of Division St the old main street continues, again with little more left than the old sidewalk. As the paved road bends left, a few more early homes are found. After a few paces the road then bends sharply right. As it does, the empty street pattern continues to be evident to the south, and the sidewalk then suddenly ends amid the weeds on the roadside. Here, on the vacant lots, formerly stood the blacksmith shop, the church and the cheese factory.

The road continues north from the forlorn village and mounts a rise. Below the hill, in the valley of Percy Creek, the bustling town of Warkworth spreads out. With its still active feed mill, its historic main street of stores and cafés, and its residential areas, it remains a busy centre for the area's rural residents.

The main street of its once potent rival, Norham, however, remains a vague and ghostly shadow of its former days.

Directions

 Norham lies on Platt Rd, just east of County Road 25 and about 25 kilometres north of Colborne.

 *Normandale*

...an early industrial town...

It won't take long to visit the main street of Normandale. There isn't much left of it. Yet for nearly two decades, from the 1820s to the 1840s, it was one of the busiest industrial towns on the Canadian shore of Lake Erie. Still, the few structures that date from those heady times, its little gully and its lakeside bluffs all give it a markedly unusual air.

It all began around 1810 with the arrival of English ironmaster John Mason at Potter's Creek, near the fledgling Long Point settlement. Having heard of the plentiful bog ore deposits in the area's swamps, he put his skills to work by building an iron smelter. However, he died before he could bring it into production and the smelter was sold to a consortium of Americans named Hiram Capron, George Tillson and Joseph Van Norman.

Capron and Tillson subsequently left to found the towns of Paris and Tillsonburg, respectively. Now under the Van Norman brothers, the iron furnace was producing many of the appliances and utensils needed by the growing local population, including cook stoves. On the wall of the gully formed by the creek, the furnace consisted of a large brick chimney 30 feet (9 metres) high, a water wheel beside the creek and a pair of bellows. Here the molten iron was poured into molds in a nearby floor. At its peak, the furnace yielded 700-800 tonnes of iron a year.

The town site consisted of the workers' cabins and two hotels with a population of 300. Van Norman ultimately sold the lots to his workers. However, by the mid-1840s, the supply of bog ore was becoming scarce, and the lumber that fired the furnaces was even scarcer. Van Norman left to try and tap the iron ore in Marmora east of Peterborough, but it proved too remote to be viable.

Although Normandale dwindled in size, it didn't completely die out. In the 1860s, John Shaw bought the furnace and built in its place a flour and grain mill. A wharf was built into the lake, and Normandale developed into a minor fishing port. But these industries, too, soon vanished.

Then yet another era began—summer tourism. A tourist hotel opened atop the bluff, and cottages soon lined the shore where the fishermen's net sheds once stood. Today the town has evolved further into a rural retreat. Yet, on its modest yet picturesque main street, vestiges of its earliest days still stand.

The most prominent building stands east of the main intersection (Main Street and Victoria Street, or Normandale Road, as it is now called). The former Union Hotel is regarded as one of the oldest wooden hotels still standing on site in all of Ontario. It dates from the heyday of the Van Norman furnace, having been built around 1833. It now serves as a bed and breakfast. The two-storey porch, removed years ago, was rebuilt during the hotel's restoration in the 1980s.

Immediately west of the hotel, and complementing it to perfection, is a diminutive structure with a boom town facade that once served as the village store and post office.

East of the Union Hotel stands another early home. Although it does not date back to the days of the furnace, the house was added in 1888 by Harvey Wilcox, a fish wholesaler. Closer to the bluff, the

The hotel and former post office date from Normandale's early days as a manufacturer of iron.

site now occupied by a trailer park once contained a popular summer hotel, the Lakeview Hotel. Built around 1920, it was destroyed by fire in 1969.

On the south side of Main Street, the brick Methodist church, built around 1870, is now a residence, while the home beside it is the renovated dwelling of an early fisherman.

From the hotel corner, Mill Street continues downhill to the site of the former mill and fish hatchery, although neither remains. No trace of the long-vanished furnace is evident here, either. A plaque commemorating the Van Norman furnace has been placed beside a small parking area, although at the time of this writing, it had gone missing. Mill Street continues to the beach area.

Immediately west of the main intersection stands another trio of early structures. The two-storey house on the northwest corner was built by Richard Ferris and dates back to the days of the furnace. On the southwest corner, the still-functioning general store was likely built sometime between 1868 and 1875, while the home east of it is more recent and dates from the 1920s.

One of Ontario's more celebrated homes stands west of the store and on the south side of the main street. This Regency cottage, with its French doors that open onto a wrap-around porch and with its square cupola, was built in 1841 by Romaine Van Norman, son of the furnace's founder. It has been frequently featured in books on Ontario's outstanding heritage homes.

A few paces west of the house, at the southeast corner of Hill St, stands a two-storey house that was once the Red Tavern, operated by James Thompson.

The main street then continues westerly to eventually rise out of the gully. Here a few early workers' homes still stand, although most of the dwellings are of more recent vintage.

Although Normandale is not a ghost town, the vestiges of its once-bustling heyday give its main street a ghostly aura of those more prosperous times.

Directions

 Normandale lies on Lake Erie about 15 kilometres west of Port Dover.

 *Palmerston*

...a railway hub...

The spark that created Palmerston's small main street has now been extinguished. Located in the central plains of western Ontario, Palmerston was pivotal in the development of a network of railway lines that led to various ports on Georgian Bay and Lake Huron. Although the trains no longer call, the one-time railway yards and large wooden station remain a visual legacy on the main street. It is a legacy that few main streets in southern Ontario share.

As the Grand Trunk Railway gobbled up the many local lines across Ontario, they needed larger yards and larger stations. After 1882, the year of its major amalgamation with the Great Western Railway and its network of lines, trains began to converge on Palmerston from six different directions: from Wiarton and Owen Sound on Georgian Bay, from Southampton and Kincardine on Lake Huron, and from key junctions at Stratford and Harrisburg, near Brantford.

The extensive sidings stretched for nearly a kilometre southeast of the main street. Midway stood the station on the southwest side of the yards, while the roundhouse stood on the northeast side. The station was a two-and-a-half-storey wooden structure with towers over one corner and over the main entrance. Tracks hugged both sides of the station building.

To allow workers and pedestrians to safely cross the yards, a long pedestrian overpass was built and, along with the station, became one of the main street's more prominent landmarks.

Palmerston's historic railway station has been restored, and the landmark pedestrian bridge preserved.

Palmerston's decline as a railway hub began in 1957 with the elimination of steam and its replacement with diesel as a fuel for locomotives. Passenger service ended in 1970 and a decade later the station was closed. Since then all train service has ended entirely, and the tracks, which once led to six different destinations, are no more.

Happily, a small number of sidings do survive, for Palmerston remains the host village for an annual handcar competition. These hand-operated jiggers were once a common sight, carrying work crews and inspectors to view and repair the tracks. Now teams from across North America compete to gain the best time along the tracks in the former yard. In the late 1990s, the station itself was restored and repainted in its original green paint scheme. The footbridge remains in place as well. At the north end of the yards stands another relic of Palmerston's railway heritage—CN steam engine 81. The three-storey Queen's Hotel, which formerly stood behind the station, has long since been replaced by houses.

The main street stores lie along William Street, which runs behind the station, and Main Street, which crosses the north end of the yards.

While no buildings of outstanding heritage or architectural merit are to be found on the main street, their architecture nonetheless reflects the simple and functional nature of most railway divisional towns. A heritage mural has been added to the side of the store at James and Main, recalling in images and words Palmerston's railway legacy. Most stores appear to date no earlier than around 1880, and none have undergone heritage facade renovations. Only the Palmerston Tavern suggests a heritage link to the time when railway workers would crowd in at the end of their shift.

Unlike other former railway hubs, such as Lindsay, where all evidence of its railway days have disappeared, Palmerston's railway heritage still plays a prominent part on its main street, even though the trains no longer call.

Directions

Palmerston lies on Perth CR91 about 45 kilometers northwest of Kitchener.

 *Perth*

...Ontario's prettiest main street...

The main street of Perth stands apart among Ontario's main streets for many wonderful reasons. Its history dates back to before the earliest days of general settlement in eastern Ontario. Laid out in a strict military grid of streets, Perth was created to act as insurance against U.S. attacks on the more vulnerable St Lawrence River settlements.

Its buildings reflect the skilled workmanship of Scottish stonemasons, who, hired to build the Rideau Canal, also created what has been called Ontario's finest stone main street. The heritage of Perth's main street is so strong that Heritage Canada made it one of its priority main streets for heritage preservation. In the year 2000, TVO's Studio Two declared it Ontario's "prettiest town".

Perth, however, needed more than a couple of mills and a population of half-pay army officers to become a viable community. That prosperity came in 1823 when it was designated the capital of the Bathurst district, a status that brought to it a courthouse, a jail and the various administrative functions needed for a district capital.

While the Rideau Canal opened up the area to commerce and settlement in 1832, it passed Perth by and it was not until 1840 that the Tay Canal connected the two. Finally, in the 1880s, the CPR laid its tracks through town and Perth developed an industrial base.

Gore Street forms the main street of Perth running north-south through the tidy old grid, and the buildings along it date largely from the period 1823-1880.

The best place to start a tour is from the parking lot in the new farmers' market adjacent to the landscaped turning basin for the Tay Canal. Here many of the main street buildings can be seen reflecting in those quiet waters. A plaque on the main street at this location displays an early sketch of the town.

Here, too, on the west side of Gore St, is the town's most prominent building, the town hall. Despite a relatively understated entrance, the 1863 stone structure gained considerably more flair in 1874 when a tall cupola was added to the roof. Its architect was John Power of Kingston. The building facing it across the street is not one of the town's oldest, but rather an art deco style post office added in 1931.

Immediately south of the post office and overlooking the turning basin stands the Doran Block, built of stone in 1840 and containing three storefronts, all well-preserved to reflect the style of that era.

South of the turning basin, at the northeast corner of Gore and Harvey, stands another distinctive commercial block. Built in 1840 by postmaster James Allan, it, too, is stone and consists of three storefronts, the middle one of which is indented and topped by a gable. The two flanking stores are extended towards the street and offer hip gable roofs.

One building that defies the Scottish stone character of the street is the McMartin House, located on the southeast corner of Gore and Harvey. Built in 1830 by Perth's first lawyer, Daniel McMartin, the brick building displays an American style of architecture known as "federalist," reflecting McMartin's New York roots.

Back at the town hall, the tour now heads north along Gore St. Just north of the town hall, at the northwest corner of Gore and Market, the former Tay Navigation Co offices were built in the 1830s.

A restaurant has taken advantage of its attractive location beside the Tay River in Perth.

Extending seven bays wide with a ground level arched doorway, it has over the years housed three ground level businesses, and, in the upper floors, offices of lawyers and barristers. It overlooks the Tay River.

Next along the west side of the road is the large three-storey flat-roofed Graham Block. What began as a two-storey stone building in 1830, with the usual sloped roof, was enlarged in 1911 to three full storeys, with the flat roof more typical of commercial buildings of that period.

Meanwhile, on the east side of Gore St, there stands a solid row of more early stone buildings, again well-preserved. One of the most distinctive however, is not one of the street's oldest; rather, it is the 1907 Carnegie Library. Here the Tay River flows between a pair of two-storey stone buildings built in the 1840s. Today, the river level basement of one is home to Mexicali Rosa's restaurant, which added an attractive waterside patio.

North of Herriott St, the east side of the main street continues to display a variety of building styles, most dating from the 1840s. This leads to another of the street's more notable buildings, the Matheson House museum. Roderick Matheson built this home in 1841, a building which also contained his store and warehouse. Its wide three bay palladium facade is flanked by a pair of wings extending to the sides. Like its neighbours, it is built of stone and extends two and a half storeys. A period garden has been planted in the small plot adjacent to the south side of the museum.

To the north of the museum and on the southeast corner of Gore and Foster are the buildings that began as Matheson's saddle and harness shop but have operated as Shaw's store since 1859. The stone buildings located behind it on Foster Street formerly housed Matheson's stable and coach house.

On the west side, opposite the museum, is an example of a bank ren-

Perth's main street beautification earned it the title of being Ontario's prettiest main street.

ovation that is sympathetic to the overall streetscape. Built in 1884 as the Bank of Montreal, it displays a mansard rood with a large gable and an arched entrance, the latter being a recent restoration. In the beginning it was described as the most elegant building in town, a description that fits even today.

North of Foster St, a cross street of other early commercial buildings, Gore St becomes residential in character. In fact, most of Perth's streets contain a treasure trove of early stone homes, churches and mills. Behind the town hall, Stewart Park provides extensive landscaped grounds through which to stroll after touring one of Ontario's more spectacular main streets.

Directions

 Perth lies on Highway 7, 80 kilometres west of Ottawa.

 *Petrolia*

...forgotten legacy of the black gold...

The elaborate architecture of Petrolia's main street takes the visitor back to a forgotten era when black gold was king and Petrolia was the royal city. In 1858 James Miller Williams dug into the oily gum beds known throughout the flat farmlands of Lambton County and brought into production North America's first commercial oil well.

With the continent in the throes of an industrial boom, oil and its products were in increasing demand. A few kilometres north of the well, Petrolia boomed as a producer of refined oil with 27 refineries. By 1861 the oil field contained more than 400 wells. Stores appeared on the main street, many built in what was known as the "Chicago style" of architecture—three storeys in height with cast iron pillars.

Within a few years two railway lines had been built into the area, the Canada Southern, which passed between Petrolia and Oil Springs; and the Great Western, to the north of Petrolia. Neither, however, ventured into the town. Exasperated, the town council built its own line to connect with Great Western. The Canada Southern followed suit by extending a branch into town from the opposite direction.

Petrolia quickly acquired homes and businesses that displayed the architectural excesses brought on by wealth. But the boom would not last. Despite its international reputation, when Standard Oil bought Imperial in 1898, the refinery was moved to the port of Sarnia, and Petrolia sank into stagnation.

North America's first commercial oil well gave rise to Petrolia and Oil Springs.

Most of the key commercial buildings line Petrolia St between Oil St and King. Here, the main focus is the town square. Facing this shady green space on the south side is the beautiful Victoria Hall. Constructed in 1889, it served as town hall, police station and fire station. However, when built, the town's residents insisted that it also include an opera house, as befitted a community of wealth. Gutted by fire, it has recently been restored.

Facing the square from the north side of Petrolia St is perhaps the main street's most unusual building, the former Grand Trunk train station. Designed to complement the town's status, it was built with a pair of circular towers at each end, and a square tower to mark the entrance. Being a "terminal" station, the tracks ended behind the building. But with the decline of the town, the railway halted its service in 1930 and the station became a civic centre. Finally, in 1937, the town bought the building from CN and converted it into a library. The interior still contains original electric light fixtures and pine floor boards. In 1975, it became the first of several buildings in town to receive a heritage designation.

West of the square, a three-storey red brick building represents the former post office, now housing commercial functions.

Several other commercial buildings still retain the glory of the oil era, which was reflected in its architecture. At number 4211-13 Petrolia St, the McKay Block, built in 1887, retains many of its original facade features, such as recessed panels, the use of decorative brickwork, and the gabled parapet with its date stone.

Number 4230 is the Oddfellows Hall. Built in 1888, it displays Italianate features such as the dominant cornice and round headed windows. Its architect, Isaac Erb, incorporated cast iron columns with floral patterns in the keystones and coloured glass in the upper windows.

One of the more delightful buildings is Diana's at 4172-4 Petrolia St. Part of a commercial block built in 1866, it is set apart by its three-sided bay window on the second floor situated immediately above a very unusual central doorway that is flanked by colourful columns of brick and stone with metal brackets.

Many other commercial buildings have the names embedded in their upper levels, including the 1892 Canneff Block and the nearby Archer Block. Even the 1911 Bank of Nova Scotia was added with extra architectural flair.

East of Oil Street lie many of the town's old mansions. A stroll south along Ella St and around Crescent Park reveals an entire crescent of mansions built by Petrolia's oil kings. And at the northeast corner of Petrolia and Oil looms the castle-like Fairbank House, named Sunnyside and built in 1890 by one of the town's leading oil magnates, John H. Fairbank.

About 10 kilometres south of Petrolia is Oil Springs, where the oil boom began in 1858 when James Miller Williams began digging into the gum beds and struck oil 4 metres down. Even though it was only pumped by hand, it still yielded oil at the rate of 50 barrels a

Petrolia's main street improvements reflect the community's oil boom heritage.

day. He then added a refinery to make kerosene and other oil products, the world's first. By the end of 1860, Williams' wells were yielding up to 400 000 gallons a year. The rush was on and Oil Springs quickly soared to a population of 3000.

Oil Springs' bubble burst in 1866 when the Petrolia fields began to produce. By 1880, Oil Springs was a near ghost town, its population now a mere 250. A few years later the fields were subdivided and sold. Gradually, the new owners brought the wells back into production, and the town slowly recovered. The village, however, has retained only meager vestiges of those heady days.

The main street, about 2 kilometres long, boasted twelve general stores, nine hotels, saloons and a road "paved" with thick planks of oak. The plank road extended all the way to Port Sarnia 30 kilometres away.

The once-booming main street seems like the ghost street it once was. Vacant lots and empty buildings tell of bygone glory. While a general store still functions near the corner of Main and Kelly, the white frame building on the north side dates from 1862 and is the former home of the *Oil Springs Chronicle*, the area's first daily newspaper. Over the years, however, most of the stores and institutions of those grand glory years have fallen victim to fire and indifference and no longer survive to celebrate that heritage.

A drive around the back lanes of Oil Springs, such as Blind Line, Kelly Road, and 18th Side Road will show many of the ancient jerker rods still creaking back and forth across the fields, allowing the pumps to bring modest amounts of oil to the surface where they are stored in tanks to await collection. Here, too, near the corner of Kelly Road and Blind Line, stands the Oil Springs Museum with the site of the world's first commercial oil well.

A driving tour, available at the museum, will unlock the unusual vestiges of Ontario's forgotten boom.

Directions

Petrolia is on Lambton County Road 21 about 30 kilometres southeast of Sarnia, with Oil Springs about 10 kilometres south

 *Port Colborne*

...a canal side stroll...

A glance at Port Colborne's historic main street, West Street, instantly reveals both its heritage and its appeal. Here, where the Welland Canal connects with Lake Erie, West Street is a canal side main street.

Settlement started in the area known as Gravelly Bay with the arrival of the "late Loyalists" around 1790. A village grew around Christian Zavitz's gristmill and became known as Petersburgh, after Peter Neff, the first settler. Sometime after, the name was changed to Humberstone.

In 1831, in anticipation of the extension of the Welland Canal from Port Robinson to Lake Erie, a harbour was cleared around Gravelly Bay. Following the opening of the new canal in 1833, the Welland Canal Co erected new gristmills near the entrance lock, then located near what are today West and Sugarloaf Streets. With ships having to tie up near the lock, West St began to develop as a commercial centre, with taverns, stores and hotels. One well-known hostelry at this location was the Lakeview Hotel.

In 1854, the face of the village changed again with the arrival of the Buffalo Brantford and Goderich Railway, which followed the shore of the lake from Fort Erie to Dunnville. It was followed in 1859 by the Welland Railway, which paralleled the east side of the canal from Port Dalhousie to Port Colborne. A station was built where the two rail lines crossed, and Fraser St, located behind the station, developed into a busy street of commerce as well.

By 1880, Port Colborne could count more than 240 houses, and factories and industries were arriving almost daily. The West St business section grew to seven blocks long, stretching from Elgin St on the north to Sugarloaf St on the south.

By the late 1880s, the Lake Erie shore was also becoming popular with vacationing Americans, whose own shorelines were now engulfed in factories. In 1888 the American-owned

Many of Port Colborne's main street stores have found new uses since the time when it reached its peak

Humberstone Club, or "Solid Comfort," developed along the lake on what is today Tennessee Ave. Many of their early grand summer homes still stand.

The enlargement of the canal in 1887 allowed for larger ocean-going vessels to pass through the canal, spurring on more industry to develop around the busy harbour. In 1908 a new government grain elevator was built to replace the obsolete Grand Trunk elevator, while in 1917 Maple Leaf Mills opened their new operation a short distance upstream. Until 1960 it remained the British Empire's largest flourmill. The government elevator was rebuilt in 1920 following a deadly explosion that killed 12 workers.

West St, Port Colborne's main street, looks over a widened Welland Canal.

Then, in 1933, the building of the wider 4th Welland Canal changed the face of the town once more. The expanded canal forced the closing of the east side railway station, and a new station was built on the west side. Then, when the old entrance lock was removed and a new lock was built a kilometre upstream, West St businesses began to stagnate. A new commercial core grew a block west around Charlotte and King Sts.

Fires took their toll on West St as well, with major blazes in 1919, 1926 and 1938, destroying many of the early stores. The discovery of gas at nearby Sherkston proved to be a mixed blessing, as many of the infernos started in the new gas stoves.

Still, Port Colborne's historic main street offers both history and boat watching as monster vessels inch along the canal. A good place to begin is at the railway station at the north end of West St. Built in 1925 in advance of the canal widening, it closed in 1977 and today has become a popular Greek restaurant. Near the station the old stonework of the earlier canals still survives as a separate channel beside the new canal. The railway swing bridge is still in place but is now trackless, as the rail line between here and Fort Erie has been abandoned. A new spur line has been built from Welland along the west bank of the canal to access the elevators in the harbour. On the east side of the canal, the former main street, Fraser St, retains only a few vestiges of the times when it was a busy commercial street by the first station.

Most of the buildings on West St have always been modest in scale and in architectural embellishments. Indeed, only one has been designated a heritage structure.

There are, however, a few buildings of note. The former L.G. Carter general store, built in 1851, did manage to survive the fires and displays an Italianate style with rounded windows and a flat roof. At 212 West St, the Imperial Bank of Canada was built in 1911 with a terra cotta exterior and in a style that is called "Italianate Classic Revival," with a dominant cornice and arched windows. At this time, the intersection of West St and Charlotte was called the "best business corner in town." That would all change a few years later.

At 118 West St, Marsh Engineering carries on a long-standing tradition of marine repairs, dating back to 1870 when it was first established as F. Woods and Sons.

The oldest building on West St is found at number 62, a house that is the former Lakeview Hotel. It was moved to this location in 1889 and converted to a captain's home. Built originally of clapboard, it contains oval windows, a two-storey bay window and a two-storey veranda, which was reconstructed following a vicious wind storm.

Many of the other businesses still in operation are situated in modest buildings, either flat-roofed brick buildings, or frame buildings with front gables. Opposite the stores on West St, a landscaped walkway follows the edge of the canal along the east side of the street.

There are other sights to be seen in Port Colborne as well. A new park by the harbour offers picnicking and boating, while the stone gates to the former Tennessee Ave enclave of "Solid Comfort" still stand and are now a designated heritage structure.

But it is the canalside main street that most strongly relates to Port Colborne's Welland Canal heritage.

Directions

 Port Colborne is situated on the shore of Lake Erie, about 25 kilometres south of St Catharines and 30 kilometres west of Buffalo.

 Port Hope

...a perfect 19th century main street...

The view from the top of the Walton Street hill is awe-inspiring. It is not a distant vista of valleys and forests, but one of a main street that many have described as a perfectly preserved example of a 19th century main street.

It's not just the historic integrity of the street that sets it apart, but also the scale of the buildings. Most are three to four storeys in height, rather than the more common two-storey structures in most commercial cores. There are also the more elaborate architectural embellishments, for much of Walton St developed during a period of relative prosperity, albeit a brief one.

The subsequent economic stagnation was one of the factors that discouraged the replacement of many of these early structures. In fact, Port Hope's population remained at less than 6000 from the 1880s until the late 1940s. With little or no growth, there was little incentive to tear down the old. Port Hope's main street also escaped the fiery fate that befell most main streets in the late 19th century, allowing many early structures to survive.

Port Hope boomed with the export trade in lumber and barley shipped in from the hinterlands and out through the port. The opening of two railway lines in the 1850s, the Grand Trunk and the Midland, brought further prosperity and many of the main street buildings date from this period.

But by the 1880s growth was slowing. The port at nearby Cobourg was bigger and better, and many of the steamers preferred to call there. Furthermore, Cobourg had been designated as the county seat. When the Americans placed a tariff on barley and when the lumber had been stripped from the hinterland, Port Hope entered a period of stagnation that would last until after the Second World War. The remarkable houses, stores and hotels of Port Hope changed little.

A fitting place to start a tour of Walton St, Port Hope's main street, is at the top of the hill. Here, the row of homes on the north side, numbers 134-136, is known as the Metcalfe Terrace. Built in 1856, these homes are elaborately embellished with a series of four pilasters, a heavy roofline, stone lintels and decorative wood trim around the doors. Their facade remains as it was when they were built.

Their neighbour, a few paces to the west, is another perfectly pre-served house, the frame "Mission Duplex". Built in 1843, it is a two-storey clapboard duplex beneath which an arched carriageway still passes.

Descending Walton Street leads to the St Lawrence Hotel on the south side. Four storeys high, it sports an Italianate motif. The 17 rows of narrow windows have cast iron heads, while the five store-fronts have been restored to their original appearance, and are sloped to match the Walton Street hill. It was the threat to demol-ish this elegant building in 1963 that awakened the populace to the beauty of their built heritage and to the possibility that it might dis-appear.

Across from the St Lawrence Hotel, the Bank of Montreal building at the northwest corner of Walton and Cavan dates from 1871 and displays the rounded corners and windows needed for its corner location.

Then, at the southwest corner of John and Walton, stands the Royal Bank. Before becoming a bank it housed a variety of village businesses, while the second floor contained the town's opera house. The tall rounded second floor windows, with pilasters between, were used to light the hall.

The Walton Hotel stands at the southeast corner of Walton and John St. Built in 1871, it was first known as the Queens Hotel and replaced an earlier 1819 hotel. The recessed doorway and the pillars at the entrance set this one apart.

East of the hotel, a narrow walkway meets Walton Street from the south. This represents the old right of way of the historic Midland Railway. While the embankment has been asphalted down to Augusta Street, the rear portion of Lent's Travel housed the former Walton St station for passengers waiting to board the trains.

The beauty of the street continues on both sides from Ontario Street to the Ganaraska River bridge. Most buildings are three or four storeys in height, many incorporating an Italianate design. Across from Queen St stands the former North American Hotel, while on the southeast corner, the Gillett-Paterson Block dates from 1845. Three storeys high with its rounded corner, it boasts six pilasters on each side, stout chimneys on the roof and rounded windows that grace its preserved ground floor facade. A glance inside some of the stores show that the owners have restored the interiors as well, in many cases revealing the original pressed tin ceilings.

As with many main streets in Ontario, the side streets offer up their treasures, too. A short distance south on Queen stands the restored Capitol Theatre. An "atmospheric" theatre, it was built in 1930, and now houses a multi-purpose arts centre.

A short distance south along John Street leads to the old Midland

The main street of Port Hope has been described as Ontario's best preserved example of a 19th century main street.

House hotel, built in the 1850s to accommodate passengers on the Midland Railway that ran past its back door. A few paces north on Ontario Street, the Ganaraska Hotel, built in 1856, was another hostelry to accommodate the railway.

The town hall on Queen St dates from 1851 and was designed by a Rochester architect named Merwin Austin. Rochester, it must be remembered, was connected by regular steamer service across the lake.

Ironically, if any town should be grateful for its failure to grow it should be Port Hope, for that era has left the town with a main street legacy unparalleled anywhere in Ontario.

Directions

Port Hope is located about 110 kilometres east of Toronto.

 *Port Perry*

...lakeside heritage...

One glance at the main street of this small lakeside town will reveal why it has become a choice location for film companies seeking historic small town main streets.

The town is the creation of the man after whom it was named, Peter Perry. A failed politician, Perry developed the harbour at Whitby before moving on to the shores of Lake Scugog to lay out a town site he called Scugog Village. His intent was to facilitate the shipping of lumber from the timberlands around Lake Scugog through his harbour on Lake Ontario.

At first, the timber was hauled from Port Perry down the Plank Road, now Highway 12, to Port Whitby. Later, it was loaded onto the trains of the Whitby and Port Perry Railway in the yards on the Port Perry waterfront.

During Port Perry's formative years, passengers and freight frequently travelled by steamer. In fact, the lake was created just for that purpose. Prior to 1829, the "lake" was no more than a wide marshy river valley. But in that year William Purdy constructed a dam in Lindsay to raise the height of the Scugog River and in so doing filled in the valley to create Lake Scugog.

The first nucleus of the fledgling village was at the corner of today's Queen St and Simcoe Rd and was known as Borelia. Seven steamers regularly called at the wharf, making other stops at Port Hoover, now a ghost town, Caesarea, and Lindsay. As shipping increased, the area around the wharf began to develop, and soon Queen St was lined with wooden stores right down to the lake.

Finally, in 1871, the Whitby and Port Perry Railway opened using a wooden station in what is today Palmer Memorial Park. More shops and businesses filled in the lots lining Queen St. Then, on the night of July 3rd 1884, a fire that began in the sheds behind McQuay's Hotel rapidly spread, and within hours the entire main street between John St and the lake was a raging inferno. Every building, except the grain elevator, was consumed in the conflagration.

Within a few months, a new main street had appeared, with stores now constructed in brick, and many displaying the architectural experimentation popular in the closing years of that century. That same main street today attracts the eye of Hollywood.

The best way to appreciate the origins of this main street is from the old concrete wharf by the lake. The view up the hill is of the brick

Movie scouts are attracted to the heritage of Port Perry's main street.

streetscape framed by the trees in the park. The vista across the lake is little altered from that enjoyed by the townspeople, who would have waited here to board the steamers to Lindsay, or the trains to Whitby. The old station itself was moved to the west side of Water St and is now a flower shop. The tracks and all other railway buildings were removed in the 1940s when the line was abandoned. The only other building that is tied to the railway era is the grain elevator beside the park, which was built in 1868 and was the only structure to survive the fire.

The lakeside has been improved over the years with a new marina and boardwalk.

Up the hill from the lake, the first key building on the main street is the former St Charles Hotel, located on the southwest corner of Queen and Water St. This three-storey brick building still boasts its mansard roof and second-storey window decorations. The ground floor facade, however, has been altered over the years.

The Brock building at number 168, by contrast, still retains its 1884 facade as well as many of the interior features. But perhaps the single most-photographed structure on the main street lies on the north side and is known as the Blong Block. Its facade has remained virtually unaltered since its construction in 1884 and is especially noted for its length and its fanciful roof parapets. The red brick is highlighted with yellow bricks around the windows and in its pilasters. It stands on the site of the Royal Arcade, a business established by one of the town's early industrialists, Joseph Bigelow, and sold in 1881 to Jonathan Blong. Today it houses the Settlement House and a variety of shops.

Back on the south side, a small open area provides benches and flowers in front of the 1912 post office. It was here that McQuay's Hotel stood before the devastating fire began in its sheds.

Constructed of red brick and grey stone, the post office clock tower visually dominates the downtown.

Between Perry and John St, several buildings reflect the architectural trends of the late 1880s. Note the detailed brick work on numbers 228, 230 and 250, and especially the gables on the latter two buildings.

The area west of John St was spared in the fire. Here, close to the corner of Simcoe St, are the Presbyterian church, which dates from 1870, and the historic Italianate town hall with its prominent corner tower, built in 1873. Along with the post office, it was once slated for demolition. However, the local townsfolk, led largely by the historical society, saved both. Much of the hall's interior has been preserved and restored, such as the staircase and balcony railings, as well as the plaster mouldings around the windows and ceiling.

It soon becomes apparent that there is more to the appeal of the main street than just the view to the lake and the architecture of many of the buildings. The business community has also worked together to coordinate store signage in a heritage motif. Overhead wires, an eyesore in many main street areas, have been removed and period street lighting has been installed. Again, it's little wonder that film location scouts like to come calling, or that the busy little lakeside avenue has become popular with daytrippers.

Directions

 Port Perry is located about 20 kilometres north of Oshawa, just east of Highway 12.

 *Port Robinson*

...vestiges of the old canal...

Once the busy terminus of the historic Welland Canal, Port Robinson today is a backwater village that clings to a few remnants of those former days of glory. And most of that legacy lies along its old main street.

Port Robinson was first laid out in 1833 as the terminus of the new Welland Canal. The original route of that vital waterway had been blasted into the earth from Port Dalhousie, south through what is today St Catharines and then up the Niagara Escarpment using a series of locks known at the time as "Neptune's Stairway." But Port Robinson was as far as it went.

At this point the canal met the Welland River, which it followed easterly to the Niagara River where ships could continue south along the swirling Niagara River to Lake Erie. Being the access point to the canal from the Welland River, Port Robinson's importance at the time outstripped that of both Buffalo and St Catharines.

Originally called simply "Beverley," it was named after John Beverley Robinson, Attorney General for Upper Canada. This important place boomed to a population of 400 and by 1850 could claim three hotels, the British Hotel, the Bells Hotel and the Mansion House. In addition, there were three stores, two blacksmiths, wagon shops, shoe shops, gristmills, a carding mill and a dry dock for the building of ships. Steam ships plied the waters to Buffalo, New York.

When the new cut was completed linking Port Robinson with Port Colborne, and with the arrival of the railways, Port Robinson swelled to a population of more than 600. A lock on the new canal was located at Port Robinson and a bridge crossed the canal to a growing community on the west side. But canal widenings and fires took their toll on the shipyard and the mills, and all have vanished with no trace.

The construction of a new Welland Canal "bypass" in 1966 removed the lock, while the railway was absorbed by the Canadian National Railway that removed the station. In 1974, the ship Steelton crashed into the bridge, sending it into the water and severing road connections between the two communities.

Although new housing and industries have swollen the boundaries of nearby Welland and Allanburg, the port's neighbour to the north, Port Robinson, has become a backwater. Its main street, once lined with stores, hotels and homes, now offers up only a few of these early structures, while vacant lots tell where the old homes and stores once stood. And it all fronts silently on the feature that gave it life and then took away that vibrancy—the Welland Canal.

Port Robinson's main street consists of South St, north of its intersection with Canby Road, and River Street, south of Canby Road. The South St portion dead-ends at a factory. But along the way, it passes several early "main street" structures. On the west side, the attractive white frame St Paul's Anglican Church dates from 1844, just eleven years after the town's beginning. A short distance farther stands the diminutive Roman Catholic church, built a number of years later. Several early frame homes also stand along this section of the main street.

Back at the intersection, on one corner, is the former Bennett Hotel, dating from 1887 and now apartments. Opposite the Bennett

Hotel, a solitary stone structure is the village's oldest building, and likely its most historic. Built originally as a tollhouse, it dates from 1830. An historic plaque has been erected beside it.

On the east side of the main street, in a large grassy park, are the remains of the old canal lock that once guided schooners and barges down the Welland Canal's first watercourse, the Welland River. A photographer's delight, its stone walls are now surrounded by high grasses and topped with bushes. The rest of the lock structure lies beneath the lawn and the road.

South of the old lock site, along the main street, a trio of early commercial buildings, including the delightfully named "Knuckleheads," is all that survives from a fire that destroyed the rest of the business section in 1888. Most of them were built circa 1850. From these early buildings, Bridge Street leads west to the site of the destroyed bridge, replaced now by a small passenger boat. Between the canal and the main street, Church St was once lined with homes and shops, but now contains only vague cellar holes and a cracked sidewalk. It took its name from the Methodist Church that once stood at the south end of the street from 1851, until it and the other buildings were levelled in 1966 to help make way for the canal widening.

South of Bridge St, many of the homes also date from early canal days and at least one is a converted hotel. An early place of business stands on the west side of the street but no longer operates. Indeed, much of Port Robinson's main street comes close to resembling that of a ghost town.

This section of Port Robinson comes to an end at the new bridge over the former channel of the Welland River. Immediately to the east of the new bridge stands the former bridge, built of concrete and now closed to vehicles. South of the crossing is the communi-

Only a trio of early stores, which once overlooked the former Welland Canal lock at Port Robinson, have survived fires.

ty of South Port Robinson, a small network of residential streets.

Lacking through traffic, the quiet village of Port Robinson is ideal for short strolls along the canal or through the vestiges of its ancient main street. Its small network of backstreets contains several old village homes and one of the first schools. The massive ocean vessels that growl past provide an often startling contrast to the little village that once was so important a place for those ships' ancestors.

Directions

Port Robinson lies at the west end of Regional Road 63 about 10 kilometres southwest of Niagara Falls.

 *Port Stanley*

...a true port...

While the main street may not be busy or architecturally renowned, it does reflect that Port Stanley is one of those rare species—an old-fashioned Lake Erie fishing port.

Its origins date back to the 1820s, when John Bostwick built a gristmill a short distance upstream from the mouth of Kettle Creek. With fertile lands being thrown open to settlement, the harbour became a busy port of entry, recording as many as 150 ship arrivals in a single year.

In 1824, the town was named in honour of a visit by a British parliamentarian, Lord Stanley. His son was to become Canada's Governor-General and the man responsible for donating to hockey the sport's oldest trophy, the Stanley Cup.

In 1856, the London and Port Stanley Railway laid its tracks into town and allowed the port to expand. Commercial fishing quickly became an important part of the town's economy, and the buildings constructed along Main Street recall that heritage.

Main Street follows the east side of the harbour from the Five Points intersection to the lake. And here your tour can start. In the middle of the five intersecting roads, an historic plaque recounts the town's founding. At the northeast corner, a flat iron building built in the 1920s has used textured concrete as its construction material. Meanwhile, on the southeast corner, the Kettle Creek Inn is one of the town's oldest inns.

The building today is an enlarged version of what began in the 1850s as a private home. In 1918 it became a hotel called the Garden Inn. It has been renovated and enlarged over the years and has become one of the more popular bed and breakfasts on the Lake Erie shore. Its green cement frogs have been a landmark of the inn for more than 60 years.

A short distance south of the inn, number 215 Main St dates from the fire that destroyed most of the street in 1854. Its board and batten facade and arched windows have remained largely unaltered, although the porch is a more recent extension. It has served variously as a town hall, a general store and a livery.

Just across James St, an interesting little side street in its own right, stands number 211, the old Russell House. Now a gift shop, it was built in the 1870s as a hotel, and has housed among other functions a bank, among whose employees was a young teller named Mitchell Hepburn, later to become a premier of Ontario.

Perhaps Port Stanley's oldest structure is number 207, known as the

A line of fishing boats testifies to Port Stanley's continuing role as a busy great lakes port.

Bostwick Warehouse. Built in 1822 by the town's founder and mill owner, John Bostwick, it was moved to this site in 1870. Although the facade has been somewhat altered, the second floor gable formerly functioned as a door for lifting items to the second floor.

Immediately beside the Bostwick warehouse, number 205 is known as the Payne House. Built in 1873 in the Gothic style, it was home to Manuel Payne, who was for a time the town's railway agent.

Meanwhile, on the opposite side of the street, a new development by the water, Inn on the Harbour, does not look at all out of place, with a style of architecture that is sympathetic to the overall appearance of the main street. Closer to the street, a small flat-roofed building is the unlikely looking former railway station for the Southwest Traction Company, which until 1918 operated streetcars from London to Port Stanley. Except for the "station," all evidence of this ancient railway has vanished. Today it houses a pet shop and a fried chicken outlet.

On the east side of the street, a few paces south of the Payne House, a small concrete block building hugs the road. Looking more like a bake oven, it was in fact a cork kiln used for drying the cork floats on fishing nets.

One of the most prominent buildings on the street is a tall three-storey wooden structure that stands on the west side. Number 194, it was added in 1917 by the East Side Fish Company. As the company was not particularly profitable, the massive building was used for many years for little more than storing fishing nets.

But to buy fish in season, a more recent building, also on the west side at the end of the street, sells fish fresh from the boats when they make their mid-afternoon return.

When the boats are not out, they can be found tied up against the long wharf, their rounded white forms sometimes numbering nearly two-dozen.

Back at the intersection, Bridge St also contains a few commercial buildings, most of more recent vintage, including the former town hall, now expanded to include the local library and theatre.

Two other nearby points of interest include the King George VI lift bridge, opened in 1937 and named in honour of the day's ruling monarch. It rises to allow boats to pass to and from the large marina a short distance upstream. A plaque on the east tower recounts the tragic loss of eight workmen during the bridge's construction.

Just across the bridge, the engine and coaches of the Port Stanley Terminal Railway await their passengers in front of the 1913 railway station. After CN closed the line in 1983, the railway has operated as a popular tourist railway with a run that has been recently extended northward to St Thomas. Beginning in 1856, it shuttled not just freight, but also passengers to this lakeside resort to dance in the famous Stork Club or simply to stroll along the long sandy beach.

But it is the main street that best recounts Port Stanley's heritage as a functioning harbour and fishing port. And there are not too many of these left.

Directions

 Port Stanley is on Lake Erie at the end of Highway 4 about 25 kilometres south of London.

 *Sparta*

...a bit of everything...

How many main streets in Ontario can offer a variety of building styles that range from Quaker to classical to Italianate, to boomtown to mud. The main street in the southwestern village of Sparta, although small, has them all.

Although American Quakers were among the first refugees from post-revolution persecutions south of the border to enter Ontario, their visual impact has been slight in most areas. This is not the case in Sparta.

The first to inspect the area inland from Lake Erie was Jonathan Doan, who had fled from Philadelphia. Here on the banks of Mill Creek he acquired more than 3000 acres and built a tannery. Other Quakers soon followed and the community grew to include mills, stores and churches. They likely chose the name Sparta after a community that many of them had been forced to leave in the U.S., although other nearby villages were adopting Greek names as well, such as Aylmer, Corinth, and Troy.

The fertile farmlands of the area attracted a flood of settlers and Sparta at its peak was a booming and promising village. While a flour and sawmill were built on Mill and Beaver Creeks, the main street would boast three hotels, three stores, a church, a school, two blacksmiths, cabinet and coffin makers and at least one tinsmith.

When the railways bypassed Sparta, the village stagnated, a circumstance that has enabled preservation of its many early buildings. With the rise in popularity of daytripping, Sparta has become a destination for residents of nearby cities such as London and Kitchener, and today many artists' studios and craft shops occupy old village shops. This trendiness happily has not diminished the architectural and aesthetic integrity of the old main street.

A large parking lot a block south of main street is the place to begin. Once at the main street, head west to see a string of early structures, most on the south side of the street. At the corner of Smith St stands the Hiram Smith store, built in 1846 to serve as a tailor shop as well as a store. Some details to note include the rare little half circle window in the peak of the gable. The bricks were all hand made.

Continuing west along the street, on the south side, the Bookshop housed in the simple frame house beside the store was the Hiram Smith family home built in 1842. The duplex just west of that is the former Dominion Hotel, constructed in 1853. The blue symmetrical house beside it was added in 1855 and served for many years as the Baptist Parsonage. The detailing around the main door is found in few other such homes. Almost as intriguing is the house next to that, the 1854 Enright House.

This then leads to a large lawn, at the back of which looms one of Sparta's larger homes, known as Ridgeview, another of the Hiram Smith family homes, this one built in 1865. Back on the street and a short distance west of Ridgeview stands one of Sparta's two mud huts. Built in the single-storey style known as the Regency style, or a square shape with a wide low roof, it was built of adobe bricks in 1830. The bricks have been covered to prevent deterioration.

West of this point the historic portion of the village gives way to newer homes.

The boomtown style tinsmith shop.

Returning to the centre of the village, you pass on the north side of the street the Baptist Church, dating from 1869, then a pair of dwellings known as "salt box" houses, so called because they resemble early salt boxes, featuring two stories at the front, with a long sloping roof line to the rear.

Then, past Smith St, on the north side, is the village's most famous structure, the old Forge and Anvil blacksmith shop. One of the oldest structures in the village, it was built in 1827 using a mixture of clay and mud. A pit was dug into a layer of clay, and then, with water and straw thrown in, trampled by oxen. The brick walls, two feet thick, remain exposed to view. Today it functions as a meeting place maintained by the local Women's Institute.

The two storey Georgian style house beside the shop was built in the 1840s and has over the years served as a newspaper office, a coffin factory and an art gallery.

Back on the south side, opposite the blacksmith shop, is another of the village's more distinctive structures, the board and batten boomtown-style tinsmith shop. It dates from the 1840s and today houses "Garden Thyme." Beside it, in turn, is the Quaker-style house built in 1838 by the owner of the blacksmith shop, John Oille, and now called "Jessa's Memories".

Closer to the main intersection, the two-storey frame house on the south side is particularly important, having been built in 1845 by Israel Doan, the son of the village's founder, Jonathan Doan. At the southwest corner of the intersection, the tall two-storey Sparta Village Suites occupies the former Temperance House. Built in the 1840s as the Sparta Hotel, it remained for many years the most bois- terous place in the village. That era ended in 1901 when the tem- perance movement bought it and banned all alcohol.

Another hotel stood across the road on the northwest corner. Built in the 1840s as the Sparta House, it displays the classic early hotel appearance, with its clapboard construction and long porch. Today it is the Sparta Tearoom. Guides to the village can be purchased here.

The tour ends at the southeast corner of the main intersection at the "Anything Used" antique gift shop. A two storey brick building with return eaves and a semi-circular fanlight beneath the gable, it dates from 1838 when Henry Yarwood built it as a general store.

Although it does not stand on the "main street," one of the village's most significant buildings, the Quaker Meeting House, lies a short distance north of the main intersection, and reflects the roots of this unusual rural village and its unique main street.

Directions

 Sparta is situated on Elgin County Road 36 about 25 kilometres south of London.

 *St Jacob's*

...an old world experience...

The main street of St Jacobs has undergone a remarkable transformation since its near-demise in the late 1960s. A predominantly Mennonite community, its businesses were losing customers to the malls and stores of the growing cities of Waterloo and Kitchener, located temptingly nearby. Today, it has been transformed into a popular destination for southern Ontario's day trippers, whether they come by car or by bus.

What they find is a main street full of shops that strongly reflect the Pennsylvania Dutch heritage of the area. Newer buildings are consistent with the architecture of the older stores, some dating back to St Jacobs' founding in the 1850s. Inside are country crafts, cuisine and quilts, most of which are indigenous to this unique area.

St Jacobs is not old by Ontario standards, or even by Waterloo-area standards. Although farmers had been arriving from Pennsylvania Dutch areas of New York and Pennsylvania since the 1780s, there was no village here on the banks of the Conestoga River before the late 1840s. When the Arthur Road opened to traffic in 1842, a stopping place for stage travellers was established where a crude wooden bridge crossed the river.

Later, Jacob Snider used the waterpower of the river to establish flour and sawmills. By 1852 Snider had created and sold several village lots and a post office was opened. As was often the custom in early Ontario, the post office adopted the name of Jakobstettel

St Jacob's main street blacksmith shop continued to shoe horses of the local Mennonites until the 1980's.

("Jacob's town"), after the village's founder. It was later anglicized to become St Jacobs.

In 1871, E.W.B. Snider upgraded the flourmill using modern technology to produce finer and whiter flour. With the arrival of a branch of the Grand Trunk Railway, more industries followed, including the O.J. Smith Shoe Company, and what is claimed to be Ontario's first creamery.

For three quarters of a century, the village served the distinctive needs of what was a largely conservative and Old Order Mennonite community. A blacksmith shop continued to function into the 1980s. But with the obvious decline of St Jacobs' economy, it fell to Milo Shantz, a descendant of early settlers, to reverse its fortunes.

In 1975 he established the Mercedes Corporation and began to revitalize failing businesses. The first was the Stone Crock Restaurant, which opened in 1975 in a converted grocery store. Then the historic flourmill, with its landmark silos, became an artists' co-op. And to avoid commercializing the Mennonite culture, the Meeting House opened to outsiders in order to convey the story and the values of the area's predominantly Mennonite farmers.

With the popularity of the Kitchener Farmers' Market nearby, St Jacobs soon became a must-see for Ontario day trippers. And it wasn't long before the conversion to a shoppers' mecca was complete. Gift and craft shops moved into the closed-up shops, while a maple syrup museum told the old way of making syrup, which is still practised on Old Order farms.

To best enjoy the main street, purchase a self-guided historic walking tour from the Meeting House. Start from the riverside parking lot behind the Riverworks Retail Centre, located in the former Canada Felting Company Factory. Here you will find booths retailing a wide range of gifts, clothing and crafts.

Opposite the Riverworks are St Jacobs' landmark silos, marking the former flourmill and now home to a wide range of artists' studios. More parking is available on Front St behind the silos. Here you can follow an unusual component of the Trans Canada Trail, a 2 kilometre footpath along the mill race that leads from the flourmill to a dam and buggy bridge.

The main street, King St, leads south from the silos past the Benjamin Inn on the east, dating from 1852 and the village's oldest place of business. On the west side stands Ontario's original Home Hardware. The first hardware store to open was Gillies in 1893. In 1934 it was purchased by Gordon Hollinger before passing into the hands of Home Hardware's founders, Walter Hatchborn and Henry Sittler.

Immediately south of the Home Hardware stands the yellow brick blacksmith shop that continued to serve the "horse and buggy" Mennonites until 1987. Today it turns out forged articles and handmade brooms. A few steps south from the blacksmith shop, the Ruffled Elegance store occupies another of the village's oldest buildings, the Steiner house, which has stood on this spot since 1857.

One notable feature of the store is the quilt-making demonstrations, often done by Old Order Mennonite ladies.

Back on the east side of the street are some of St Jacobs' more popular haunts, the Stone Crock Bakery, which features such Mennonite recipes as Dutch apple pie. Freshly bottled maple syrup is available here as well. Next to it is the Stone Crock Restaurant, the place that is credited with starting the turnaround, and The Meeting Place, where books and videos relay the culture of the area.

At the northwest corner of King and Spring Streets, A Gift to Remember occupies a former shoe store, which was built in 1860. A short distance along Spring St, the antique market has taken over the O.J. Smith shoe factory. On the southwest corner of Spring and King, Angel Treasures has moved into a former harness shop.

The northwest corner of King and Cedar has a collection of eating places, as well as a shop featuring an extensive year-round selection of Christmas ornaments. South of Cedar are more gift shops of recent construction. Not too surprisingly, many of them feature popular Mennonite quilts. At the southeast corner of King and Cedar, the former police station is now home to a gallery and studios of renowned local artist Roger Witmer.

Some of the back streets west of King lead to grander homes of the village's early business elite, including a trio of homes belonging to the Snider family, while a short drive south on King leads to the popular new home of the St Jacobs' farmers' market.

Directions

 St Jacobs is situated on Highway 86, 5 kilometres north of Waterloo.

 *St Mary's*

...stone town's main street...

Some main streets stand out for both the beauty of their buildings and the material with which they are constructed. The labels given to St Mary's—"stone town" and Ontario's "prettiest town"—give an indication of what makes this main street special.

In 1841, the Canada Company, responsible for selling land in Huron and Perth counties, put up for sale 337 acres along the north branch of the Thames River. Recognizing the waterpower opportunities of the fast flowing river, James and Thomas Ingersoll bought the parcel and immediately laid out a town site.

By 1848 the first mills were in operation and St Mary's was well on its way to becoming the milling centre for the region. In 1857, the Grand Trunk Railway built a small stone station a few kilometres north of the village on its main line to Sarnia. In the 1880s, following the amalgamation of the Grand Trunk with its main rival, the Great Western Railway, the new railway giant extended a branch line south through St Mary's to link with its newly acquired line in London. At the same time they added a new station beside the town's main street. With the railways came more industries. As the limestone bedrock was so close to the surface in the river valley, several quarries began operation, supplying stones for the construction of the buildings in this fast growing mill town.

By 1871 the population had soared to 3000 and was neck and neck with Stratford. But Stratford was named the county town and the

Grand Trunk Railway's regional headquarters, and boomed beyond anything St Mary's could ever hope for. A century later St Mary's population was only a mere 4000.

It was during the boom years of the 1870s to the 1890s that St Mary's acquired many of the stunning stores and businesses that line much of the main street even to this day.

Because many an early traveler arrived by train, the second Grand Trunk station is a fitting starting point for a tour of the town's main thoroughfare.

Located below the Queen St railway bridge, this turn-of-the-century brick station has been restored to include a tourist information office in addition to the VIA Rail waiting room. On the south side of the bridge, the stone water tower is often considered to be the town's landmark.

Although the greatest concentration of commercial buildings does not begin until Church St, a few blocks west, some impressive structures appear before that. A short distance west of the station, at 252 Queen St, a two part stone house consists of an "Ontario Gothic" style cottage built in 1849, with a larger Italianate addition dating from 1869. The enclosed porch on the latter and the open porch on the former display highly decorative patterns and fretwork.

A few steps further west, an 1850s-era limestone store still stands with a residence above. On the north side, an 1870s-store was built, unlike many of the town buildings, out of wood. From this vantage point on the hillside, the main street lies below.

The central core of the main street in effect begins with one of the most stunning town halls in southwestern Ontario. Designed by George Gouinlock in 1891, it was built with a "lasting and permanent character," according to the town councillors, "not for now, but for years and generations to come." The style is a combination of Romanesque and Italianate and its bell tower is said to be a copy of the Santa Croce tower in Florence, Italy.

For the next two and a half blocks, stores that are both simple and elaborate, some built of brick, although most of stone, are crammed together. The 1850s store at number 166 on the south side may be of particular historic interest to inveterate shoppers, as it was here that an entrepreneur named Timothy Eaton opened his first store. He remained from 1861 until 1869, when he decided to try his luck in a place called Toronto.

Numbers 158-154 house a group of stores, primarily brick, which retain their stain glass windows and decorative wooden cornices. Next to them, number 150 is one of the town's few hotels remaining out of the 17 it once had. Dating from the 1870s, its tin ceiling can still be seen in the entrance.

Between the hotel and the corner of Wellington St is another string of simple stone stores. One of them is the former Journal-Angus building, where the town newspaper began publishing in 1895.

On the north side of the street, numbers 161 and 155 are two more examples of appealing early stores, the latter of stone, and the former using decorative brick. Number 147, while offering nothing grand architecturally, was until 1890 operated by Timothy Eaton's brother, Robert.

The highlight of this part of the main street looms up on the north side at number 135. This remarkably elaborate building, especially for its size, displays its original bombé glass and wood trim on its ground floor facade, carved stonework around the windows of the second floor, and mansard roof with Gothic cornices. The whole affair is topped off by an elaborate clock tower. Fittingly, it was built originally by jeweller William Andrews in 1884, and is still occupied by a jeweller.

Between Wellington and Water Streets, more stone buildings continue to line the road, including one of the town's oldest, number 115, built in 1855. On the south side, numbers 120 through 132 all date from the 1850s, when the river was the centre of industrial activity. All are stone, with most of them being the work of T.B.Guest, the town's first reeve. Note the tin ceiling in the Stonetown Florist.

The commercial block of stores at the southeast corner of Queen and Water, all stone, still retain their wood doors and wood trim. On the northwest corner, a collection of stone stores date from the mid-1850s, and include the gabled house built by William Veal Hutton, an early mill owner.

However, the most stunning grouping of stone buildings is on the intersection's southwest corner. Premier among them is the former opera house. With its towers and crenellated roofline, it could be something right out of medieval England. A Gothic entrance and six high Gothic windows and another row of eight smaller windows on the third level complete the image.

It was designed by Silas Weekes and built in 1879-80 by the Oddfellows organization. But perhaps it was too much for the town, for it ultimately proved uneconomic to operate and was sold in 1904 to become a flourmill. Ironically, it was saved from demolition by another service organization, when it was rescued in 1987 by the Lions and converted to apartments.

Opposite the opera house, the limestone post office, dominated by its Dutch gable, was added in 1907. It is now a pub.

St Mary's opera house, now apartments.

Your tour really should end where the town began, at the river. Here the historic Victoria Bridge carries Queen St across the shallow Thames. One of Ontario's oldest surviving in-use bridges, the stone structure was built in 1865. In the 1980s, it had deteriorated to the point where the town council voted to demolish it. However, heritage won the day, and the bridge was rebuilt instead. It is the province's second longest stone bridge, bested only by the five arch stone bridge at Pakenham.

Beside the bridge, an old millrace has been preserved, along with the 1910 mill wheel from the Ingersoll mill. The vista from the west side of the bridge, encompassing the stone arches and the buildings that surround it, serves to confirm that "stone town's" main street is one of Ontario's most unusual, and one of its most beautiful.

Directions

St Mary's can be found just off Highway 7, less than 40 kilometres northeast of London.

 *Stratford*

...a main street stage...

The southwestern Ontario city of Stratford is known worldwide for its yearly Shakespearian festival. While there, aficionados of the Bard may find themselves wandering around one of Ontario's more unusually shaped main streets and gazing at its centrepiece, its massive and strange looking city hall.

Stratford was a creation of the same Canada Company that developed Guelph and Goderich. The company's mandate was to open up for settlement farmlands in the Huron and Perth areas. The main settlement road began at Guelph and led to Goderich on the shores of Lake Huron. But a town was also needed between the two, and on the banks of what was then called the Little Thames River, they laid out a town called Stratford. One of the first tavern owners fittingly named his pub the Shakespeare Inn.

Despite having waterpower for mills, the village's growth was slow. Its rival, St Marys, seemed ready to become the more dominant of the two places. Then fate smiled on the muddy little place. First, it was chosen over St Marys as the new county seat. That brought with it the band of bureaucrats and businesses that an administrative centre needed. Soon railways arrived, three of them, and a further boom followed. But the most significant stimulus came in 1871 when the Grand Trunk Railway chose Stratford as the location for its major locomotive construction and repair shops.

The population quickly doubled and by 1874 topped 6000, and the railway remained Stratford's economic mainstay for three quarters of a century. Then, when the shops closed in the early 1950s, Stratford's economy slumped. However, the timely creation of the Shakespearian festival in 1953 proved to be the catalyst that the town needed to recover, and today the main street is lined with restaurants, cafés and gift shops that cater to throngs of theatre-lovers.

While the town's main thoroughfare is Ontario Street, along which Highways 7 and 8 both funnel an endless string of noisy trucks, look half a block south to find the unusual triangular main street network that rings the looming city hall a block away. The triangle consists of Wellington St, Downie St and Market Place.

Located on the northwest corner of the triangle is the Gordon Block. Although it is now used as a small mall with various business offices, the block clings to its architectural features such as Romanesque windows and pilasters.

The west side of the triangle, Wellington Street, is dominated with buildings that formerly served as hotels. Most of them date from the 1870s and were built following the boom in railway jobs. Number 22-26 is the Easson Block and until 1913 housed the Cabinet Hotel. The four-storey structure features arched windows and pilasters.

Beside the Easson Block is the Brandenburger Block, which dates from 1870. It too began as a hotel, and gradually expanded over the following decade. It features Gothic keystones and sandstone windowsills. Number 38-46, the Worth Block, began as yet another hotel, the Worth Hotel. Its three and a half storeys display the popular Gothic style and a hipped roof that still retains patterned slate shingles. Chimneys, dormers and palladian windows all remain intact.

Stratford's unusual city hall is the centre piece of the town's triangular main street.

Continuing along Wellington, number 48-50, with its yellow brick, projecting piers and cornices, also functioned as a hotel into the 1920s. Number 50-58, white with light green trim, also served as a hotel but has lost some of its early features.

The south side of the triangle is Market Square and features shops rather than hotels that tend to date from the 1890s. While the first, number 49-53, has had its most interesting feature—its two-toned brickwork—painted over and its windows altered, its roof still has the original slate.

Note the arches and decorative brick on Number 43, the original pilasters on number 41, and the unusual semi-circular windows, as well as original detailing around the doors and storefront, on number 33-37. Number 19 displays end blocks capped by decorative finials, arches and columns. Number 9 has nicely restored the original storefront, while number 1, at the corner of Downie, has a sunflower design in its bracketing and an original corner door.

Downie St makes ups the third, or east side of the triangle. The oldest building on the square stands at number 96-100. Built in 1867, it served as a hotel and sports unusual brackets. Most of the remaining buildings on this side are of more recent construction and lack the heritage of the other two sides. The Avon Theatre dates from 1901, but was redone in 1967 to accommodate more Shakespeare, as the festival was rapidly gaining in popularity at this time. The seats are original.

Further north, the Myers Block, at number 67-71, dates from the 1870s. One of the more striking structures around the square, it features a prominent corner tower, intricate brickwork and a variety of window styles that remain unaltered from its construction. Note the detailed design work along the eaves. Next to it, number 53 also displays some decorative brickwork, while number 47 is one of the few art deco buildings on the square.

The remarkable city hall is by far the dominating feature of the main street area. Its eight-sided clock tower soars five storeys above the street. The main building itself is comprised of a pair of twelve-sided wings that flank the entrance, while the back side of the hall is octagonal in shape. The main portion of the building is two storeys high, yet each of its many corners is topped by smaller eight-sided towers and punctuated by Dutch gables and small domes. A larger Dutch gable rises above the main entrance.

The building creates an overwhelming presence in what is an otherwise architecturally modest market square, and makes for one of Ontario's more unusual streetscapes.

Directions

 Stratford lies on Highway 7/8 about 50 kilometres west of Kitchener.

 *Toronto*

...the forgotten main street...

Ask anyone what Toronto's "main street" is and the answer will almost certainly be "Yonge St." That, however, would only be partly true. It certainly is the city's busiest pedestrian thoroughfare, and is touted as being the longest street in the world.

There was once a time, however, when Toronto's main shopping street was King St East. In 1856, an English visitor described it as "one of the finest streets in America...comparable to Regent St in London." Others called it the "Broadway of York."

When John Graves Simcoe, then governor of Upper Canada, laid out York in 1793, it consisted of a mere 12 streets, the most important being Front. At that time King St was known as "Duke" St. As the fledgling village began to grow, more and more shops appeared along King. They were attracted by the street's proximity to the wharves on the nearby lakeshore, and the fact that it was the main route out of town, becoming Kingston Rd as it crossed the Don River.

Finally, by the time Toronto gained city status in 1834, King St was lined with upscale shops, several hotels and taverns, stretching from Yonge St to today's Parliament St and beyond. And it retained that role until Robert Simpson and Timothy Eaton chose the intersection of Yonge and Queen Streets for their newfangled "department" stores. New businesses quickly became drawn to Yonge St and King St began to fade.

Regrettably, many of the lovely early buildings had been lost in an inferno in 1849 that raged around King, Adelaide, Church and Jarvis. Despite all the changes, a stroll today along this forgotten main street still yields a few relics of its golden heyday when all of Toronto came here to shop.

Start your tour at the King St subway station and wander east. A belated nod to the street's fading glory is the wonderful King Edward Hotel, located a few paces west of the subway. When it was built in 1901, its design by Toronto's leading architect, E.J. Lennox, ensured that it would be Toronto's most prestigious hotel. Lennox deliberately patterned it upon the Waldorf Astoria Hotel in New York, with an oak-panelled men's smoking room later known as the "Oak Room." Like its inspiration in New York, the King Edward also became the focus for entertainment in Toronto.

Between Toronto St and Church St lay the courthouse area. The open square extended north to Adelaide and consisted of the courthouse and matching jail, both built in 1824. Later, shops were extended along King, effectively eliminating the square, leaving the courthouse to face onto Adelaide. Thus, when a new courthouse was built in 1851, it fronted Adelaide St and not King. Its architect was William Cumberland, and it consisted of four Doric columns that extended three storeys high.

Although the jail and the gallows are long gone, the name lingers on in the Court House Square, now a parking lot situated behind the Adelaide Court Theatre, the current tenant of this historic structure.

Back on the south side of King stood what would in any era be a grand and elegant building, Victoria Row. A series of five shops, the building stretched five storeys high to a central tower capped with a mansard roof. Two stores of four storeys each flanked the central tower. Arches capped the third floor windows. Dating from 1842, the building was considerably upgraded in 1866 and became one of the street's most beautiful buildings.

Then in 1898 the Albany Club altered it while other sections were replaced with newer buildings. Today only one-fifth of its facade survives as Oriental Carpets.

By contrast, much of the earlier streetscape between Church and Jarvis Streets has survived. In 1849, English architect Frederic Cumberland designed the soaring St James cathedral, the fourth church on the site. Built to replace one destroyed in the 1849 fire, he designed it specifically to fit the foundations of the earlier structure. In all of North America only the spire of St Paul's church in New York soars higher. It stands on the north side surrounded by a wide lawn.

The south side is dominated by early commercial buildings. A row of four nearly identical stores stretching from the southeast corner of Church are particularly typical of the style that dominated the street in its glory years, and are among the few to have survived the great fire of 1849. Mid-block, a building with a pair of wide arched windows that stretch three storeys high marks one of Toronto's most acclaimed early commercial buildings, known as the Army and Navy Store. A dramatic contrast to its simpler but older neighbours, it was built in 1887 and represents a more fanciful era in commercial architecture.

Each window formerly had central doors and represented two separate stores. Modelled after London's "army and navy stores," it specialized in carrying top lines of men's and boy's clothing. Today it houses an accounting firm.

A row of buildings from King St's glory days.

But the grandest building on King St East, one that has become its landmark, is the domed St Lawrence Hall, dominating the southwest corner of King and Jarvis, just as it has for more than a century and a half. Taking advantage of the 1849 fire to replace the aging market building, the city commissioned architect William Thomas to design a grand hall to accommodate the many balls and gatherings that marked the social life of the era.

It is dominated by its triple arched entrance, upon which rest four Corinthian columns, a wide dormer and its familiar domed cupola. Its main hall is flanked by two wings, giving a total width of 15 rows of windows. The second floor opened out into a grand ballroom where one of the first performances was given by the diva of the day, Jenny Lind. Although, unbelievably, it was threatened with demolition in the early 1960s, saner heads, led by architect Eric Arthur, prevailed and instead it was extensively restored in 1967 as a centennial project.

On the south side of King, east of the St Lawrence Hall, those stores numbered 167 through 185 all display the simple Georgian style typical of the pre-fire shops. Although mansard rooves were added to some in later years, experts consider this to be the oldest surviving row of commercial buildings in Toronto.

East of George St one of King Street's early hotels has managed to survive, although no longer as a hotel. Number 187 still shows the simple grandeur of what was once the Nealan or Little York Hotel. With its small tower, it is the home of the Anthenium Gallery.

On the northeast corner of Jarvis, a row of restored commercial structures was built in 1850 to replace some of the many buildings razed in the 1849 fire. Their five storeys with offices and flats above the stores were almost a skyscraper beside their more typical two and three storey neighbours.

Straddling George on the northwest side of King, the former Sovereign Bank dates from 1907, while on the northeast corner George Brown College occupies what was the Christie Biscuit factory, built between 1874 and 1914. Both arrived in an era when King St was changing irreversibly from being a main shopping street to one of industries and warehouses.

Near the corner of Sherbourne, a few more early buildings survive. At number 251, the former Terry Hotel once stood. Beyond this point the old main street gives way to factories and warehouses that arrived in the late 1800s. The 20th century brought with it more changes to the streetscape, the most prominent of which is the Toronto Sun newspaper building, occupying what was once the site of the famous York Hotel.

However, a few more paces east past the Sun building is a group of exceptional old structures clustered around the intersection with

St Lawrence Hall is King St's most prominent landmark, and dates from its main street days.

Berkeley St. Once known as Parliament St, the street was renamed after the sprawling Berkeley House that faced King. This grand home, one of York's first, eventually became a warehouse before its demolition in 1925. It stood on the south side of King beside the Reid building. Upper Canada's first legislature was located at what is now Berkeley and Front. That no formal heritage recognition is given this, one of the province's most historic sites, is a sad testimony to the low regard in which the provincial and municipal governments hold this heritage.

Although a later industrial addition to King St, the Reid Lumber Company building, on the southwest corner of King and Berkeley, is one of the area's most captivating structures. To advertise its range of products, the Reids designed each window in a different architectural style, ranging from Gothic to Romanesque to Queen Anne, all embellished with fanciful detailing.

Meanwhile, on the northwest corner there survives a row of early stores, originally built by Charles Small in 1845. On the northeast corner the Garibaldi House was one of the last taverns in town before King St bent to the northeast to become Kingston Rd. It dates from 1859.

Finally, although they did not form part of King St's commercial heyday, a pair of buildings east of Parliament St do provide a fitting finale to this lost main street. They include the Little Trinity church on the south side east of Parliament, and behind it the Enoch Turner schoolhouse. While the school dates from 1848 and was Ontario's first true "public" school, the church is even older, having been built in 1845.

A short stroll to the south leads to the former Gooderham and Worts distillery complex, the oldest grouping of industrial buildings to survive in Ontario. It is being restored as part of a condominium development.

Even though Toronto is blessed with a tremendous variety of commercial streets that reflect the city's varied cultures and tastes, King St East is the only one that can truly claim to be Toronto's first real main street.

 # Townsend

...a failed dream...

There's something missing on Townsend's main street. There are no people, there are no stores, and there is no street. Townsend is one of those government dream cities that never got off the ground. Or at least, it didn't get very far.

Urban sprawl is no recent phenomenon, despite the messages that current government communications plans try to spin. Way back in the 1970s, concerned over rampant uncontrolled growth in the Toronto and Hamilton areas, the provincial government of William Davis concluded that a network of new cities, which were properly planned and modernly designed, would deflect growth pressure away from the big cities.

New cities were accordingly planned for places like North Pickering, Edwardsburg Township in eastern Ontario, and in the township of Townsend, southwest of Hamilton. While the former two got no further than the land assembly stage, construction did begin at the latter.

The plan was for a modern-looking city of 100,000 residents. Four-lane avenues, or "parkways," would wind through the city. There would be tree-lined trails for hikers, horseback riders and cross-country skiers. High schools, hospitals and shopping centres would all be connected by public transit. But the showpiece would be its town centre, its "main street."

What was to have been Townsend's showpiece town centre is largely empty and windswept.

Overlooking a landscaped pond, it was to be a complex of department stores, restaurants, cinemas, even an art gallery and a hotel. Green corridors would lead out from the town centre into all parts of the vibrant new community. By 1978, the first phase was completed and 5000 residents moved in. A wide four-lane roadway was started, the walkways were in place, and the modernistic town centre begun. But there it stopped.

What went wrong? Primarily, the jobs that were to have attracted all these new residents failed to materialize. To complement the new town, a new industrial complex had been planned for the shore of Lake Erie, a few kilometres south. But with Ontario in the grip of a recession, only three industries showed up and with only a fraction of the jobs. The dream of Townsend was over.

No part of the failed town illustrates that better than the main street. Planned in a 1970s suburban style, the main street is more like a mall than a street. The complex of attractive buildings is somewhat reminiscent of a conference resort centre with its wood trim and varied sloping rooflines. A landscaped parking lot is located on the north side, while an open square marks the south side and overlooks the centrepiece of the town centre, the pond.

Despite the well-conceived layout, the failed dream is evident everywhere. The square is largely unused, the picnic tables and benches are faded and peeling. The pond is overgrown with bulrushes, and the steps that lead to it have, in places, been roped off. The little wharf where boats were to tie up is cracked and weedy. Walkways lead away from the town centre through landscaped parks, but many now are overgrown and end in the bushes where homes were to have been.

Nor does the town centre complex have any stores. Rather it houses community facilities, such as the municipal social service department and "Reach Haldimand Norfolk."

What was to have been the town's main artery, the Keith Richardson Parkway, is four lanes of landscaped and boulevarded asphalt that extends less than a third of a kilometre before becoming a two lane farm road. The vacant land around the town site shows the start of cement curbs and roads, but these all end in overgrown fields after just a few metres. On the highways that pass by in the area, faded signs still announce the lots for sale, as they have for a quarter of a century. But the signs are as faded as the dream. And that is no better illustrated than in Townsend's "main street."

Directions

 To reach Townsend, follow Nanticoke Creek Parkway west from Highway 6 about 40 km southwest of Hamilton.

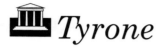 *Tyrone*

...a living museum...

Just about the entire village of Tyrone is strung out along its main street. But what sets this community apart from nearly every other place of similar size is its historic authenticity. Most of its early key buildings remain in place from the village's 19th century heyday, some still in their original use.

Tyrone began as a mill village to serve the farm population, of the fertile plains below the Oak Ridge Moraine, and was one of many similar settlements.While most of the others lost their mills, their blacksmiths and other pioneer businesses, Tyrone's main street has managed to hang on to them. That such a well-preserved village main street lies within the shadow of the rapidly sprawling GTA makes it that much more surprising.

The place to start is at the Tyrone mill. This wooden mill was erected as a gristmill in 1846 by James McFeeters. It was then bought by the Vanstones and sold in turn to Thomas Goodman, whose family ran it until 1953. While it has been much reduced in size, now less than half its original extent, it continues to operate on waterpower. In the late 1950s it was converted from a gristmill to a sawmill, and the water continued to pulse through the millrace. More recently, the grinding equipment has been reactivated.

Lumber is cut both for local construction, and for handmade furniture. Today the mill is widely advertised as a tourist attraction where freshly made doughnuts and apple cider attract visitors from a wide area. Its scenic location on a narrow road, tucked into a shallow valley, makes it popular with photographers. Its mill pond is now considered to be a local wildlife refuge.

The rest of the village lies to the east above the valley walls. A short distance east of the mill is the two-storey Vanstone house. What appears to be rectangular cut stone construction is simply stucco that has been specially shaped to give it that appearance.

Located a short distance further east, and on the south side of the road, is the unusual schoolhouse. Built in 1892, to replace the original school, which burned, the belfry soars high atop a prominent gable above the arched entrance. Although the interior has been remodeled to serve as a home, the exterior retains its original appearance.

Close by, also on the south side, another brick house began life as a Bible Christian Church in 1870. It was converted in 1885 to a residence and retains little of what could be called a church-like appearance.

The main street also contains several period homes, in particular a pair on the north side that are only slightly altered examples of the simpler village homes typical of the 19th century.

A few steps further east, at the village's main intersection, are two more of Tyrone's outstanding key buildings. Dominating the northwest corner is Byam's General Store. It was built originally as a hotel in 1855. But when the temperance movement ended its days as a tavern, it was converted to a general store. In 1895 it was bought by Frederick Byam, and today is operated by his grandson. The exterior of the structure has remained unaltered with its white wood siding and small balcony in front of the second floor door.

A visit inside will reveal that here too the past lives on. Floors,

Tyrone's 1846 mill still operates on water power

shelves, the lighting and even the arrangement of items for sale appear as they might have in Fred Byam's day.

On the northeast side of the same corner, the village smithy stands. Constructed of stone in 1856, it remains basically unchanged, from its small pane windows to its wrought iron hinges. Although horses no longer come to be shod, it did operate until 1950 as a blacksmith shop.

Then, as if to confirm the authenticity of this country treasure, the view from the store and blacksmith extends east and north over rolling farm fields. One only hopes that the relentless march of urban sprawl is a long way in the future.

Directions

Tyrone is located on Liberty St about 15 kilometres north of Bowmanville.

 Unionville

...a heritage oasis...

The main street of Unionville may be one of the most picturesque examples of an intact mid-19th century village main street in Ontario. And its gently curving orientation simply enhances its photogenic qualities.

Unionville's origins nearly predate those of Toronto, or York, as it was first called. In 1794 William Berczy led a flock of disillusioned settlers from New York State into the forests bordering the Rouge River in Ontario. South of the border these German immigrants had been promised land on which to farm but were offered instead only tenancy, and they turned to Canada for a better life. One of the arrivals, Phillip Eckardt, built a sawmill on the river where it crossed the 6th Line. Here a small string of buildings extending north from the mill constituted the first, as yet unnamed, Unionville. In the 1840s more mills were built south of Eckardt's, including Ira White's Union Mills.

While the 6th Line was the surveyed road from the village to Union Mills, it led through a marsh and had to be curved to the west to avoid the wetland. Meanwhile, the name of the mills was adopted by the first post office as "Unionville." By 1870 the settlement could claim three hotels, six general stores, a flourmill, a sawmill, and a population of 250.

In 1871 the rails of the Toronto and Nipissing Railway were laid through the village and a simple board and batten station was built at the south end of the main street. A number of industries were located near the tracks, including a planing mill built in 1873, while in 1900 the Stivers Brothers added a grain mill.

For nearly a century Unionville's main street continued to provide service to a largely rural community. But the 1950s and '60s marked the arrival of the auto age, and the beginning of urban sprawl. The first major change to the street was the loss of its stately maples and elms to make way for more parking spaces. As the urban fringe crept closer, it was proposed to widen the main street to four lanes, an action that would have destroyed its ambience and many of its heritage buildings.

Concerned citizens rallied to protest the widening and began a festival to publicize the cause. Happily, activism won the day, and a bypass was built to the east instead. This far-sighted action allowed for the preservation of one of the GTA's best heritage main streets.

Like many arriving 19th century travellers, the station is the place to start your stroll. The only station to occupy the site since 1871, it was built of board and batten, with no architectural embellishment, not even an operator's bay window. There was one door for the passengers and another for the freight. Today the Town of Markham has largely restored the building, although at this writing weeds and shrubs have obscured much of the trackside facade.

Beside the station, another unlikely survivor is the Stiver feed mill. While most such buildings have vanished from Ontario's railway landscapes, the Town of Markham has again stepped in to help preserve this key element of the village's heritage landscape.

On the east side of Main Street close to the station stands a large complex of gift shops looking much like an old mill might look. What is called the Unionville Planing Mill Complex is in fact a recent recreation of the 1854 Eakin Planing Mill, which sadly burned in 1983.

Unionville's historic main street was saved from a potentially devastating road widening thanks to a communiy effort.

Moving north up main street, you will pass several early commercial buildings and houses, a few of which date back to the 1830s, although most were built following the arrival of the railway. For example, the board and batten shop at 142-4 began as a home built in 1870. On the east side of the street, number 145 is another simple board and batten home, but this one goes back to 1845. Although a residence for most of its existence, it briefly served as the village jail.

Continuing on the east side, numbers 147 and 149 were built in 1860 and 1847, respectively, the former as a store and the latter as the Congregational church, although today it houses a shop and restaurant. Another church on the west side of the street, at the northwest corner of Varley Road and Main Street, is the elegant former Presbyterian church. The lovely stone and brick building with its slender spire was built in 1879 and may have been designed by Toronto's leading architect and the designer of Casa Loma and City Hall, E. J. Lennox. Today it serves as a veterans' meeting hall.

North of the church at number 150 stands yet another Gothic style board and batten building. Built in 1860 it served as general store, post office and taxidermy. Beside it stands the one-time Brown's General Store at 156 followed by the 1853 home of Hullet Eckardt at 158, a storey-and-a half brick home set back from the street.

Back on the east side, number 159 represents the home and hardware store of John Eckardt and was built in 1874. Much of it was rebuilt following a fire in 1977. The slender Gothic style building to the north at 161 dates from 1880 and was both the home and business of Thomas Mcdowell. For a time it also contained the Unionville Library. A nearly identical building stands across the street at 162, dating from 1865.

Then come two of the main street's more prominent buildings, the Gottlieb Eckardt wheel and carriage shop and the Queens Hotel. Both are on the west side. The two-storey brick carriage shop was built in 1835 and is one of Unionville' oldest commercial businesses. Today it contains a gift shop. Next to it stands John Webber's Queens Hotel, erected in 1871 to accommodate travellers on the newly-opened railway. It stands two and half storeys with a mansard roof and brick walls. It has been renovated and contains an ice cream shop and other retail outlets.

Across the street, number 177-9, is the former harness shop of John Devlin, although the many additions have greatly altered its original appearance. Unlike its commercial neighbours, number 187, on the east side, was a simple worker's cabin, a rare surviving example of what was once a common home in 19th century Ontario. It dates from 1850. The restaurant beside it began as a blacksmith shop in 1870, and served variously as a garage and theatre. It is one of a small number of stores on the main street to display a boomtown facade.

On the west side the adjoining numbers 192 and 194 date from around 1850 and the latter may have contained Unionville's first post office. A general store for most of its existence, today it is a café. It, too, boasts the boomtown storefront, a popular architectural device to give small buildings added grandeur. This is also the case with number 193 on the east side, which dates from 1875 and was well known as Hannah Reid's dress shop.

A few paces north of the dress shop stands the village's most unusual building, and one that is provincially significant. Known as the Salem Eckardt house, this board and batten two-storey house displays a Gothic dormer and elaborate fretwork. During the 1950s, while owned by Donald and Kathleen McKay, it was also home to renowned Group of Seven artist Fred Varley, who died here in 1969.

Facing the Salem Eckardt house is yet another Eckardt house, a two-storey fieldstone house built by Dr. Thomas Eckardt in 1872. At number 198, it is today the Old Country Inn.

Several buildings that huddle close to Carlton Road at the north end of the commercial core all originated as homes. On the east side, numbers 201, 205 and 209 date from 1907, 1870 and 1845, in that order. Meanwhile, on the west side, at number 205, Fern Cottage is the village's oldest surviving structure. Philip Eckardt, an original Berczy settler, built this home in 1829, and it is the village's only direct connection to the first days of the settlement.

A visit to Unionville any summer weekend will reveal how popular Ontario's main street heritage can be. Although parking areas have been created behind the east side of the main street, and at the corner of Carlton, it can take time to find an available spot, especially during the annual festival. This is the same festival that began the effort to preserve this rare and walkable village main street.

Directions

 Unionville's historic main street lies in the Town of Markham, north of Highway 7 between Warden Ave and Kennedy Rd.

 *Vittoria*

...a capital place...

Few today have heard of a little community, just north of Lake Erie, called Vittoria. Yet for a brief decade in the early 19th century, it was the most important place in southwestern Ontario.

And the old main street still harbours vestiges of that lost legacy.

When the district of London was created in 1801, a place was needed for its administration. Facilities would include a courthouse, a jail and offices for the usual bureaucrats. A town site would be required for the judges, the employees of the court and the shopkeepers. The first location to be picked was Charlotteville high atop a bluff overlooking Lake Erie.

After the War of 1812 the site was moved to Tisdale's Mills, a short distance inland. Almost immediately it was renamed Vittoria to celebrate a victory by the British at a town of that name during the Napoleonic wars.

In 1815, Vittoria built its new courthouse, measuring 40 feet (12 metres) long and 26 feet (8 metres) wide. The courthouse also was home to the London District School and the Masonic Lodge.

A town plan was devised with the courthouse occupying a square in the center. The town had two hotels, including the Steamboat and Stage House, which had been built as early as 1804. Several large homes of brick and wood were built by various district officials.

In November of 1825, following a meeting of the Masons, the courthouse burned to the ground. Rather than rebuild in Vittoria, the government of Upper Canada chose instead the site that Governor Simcoe, Upper Canada's first governor, had initially selected as the provincial capital, London. In the 1870's Vittoria could boast mills, a cannery, a cheese factory, several stores, and the Catherwood and Tuttle Hotels.

And so, following its brief day in the sun, Vittoria settled into becoming just another of the many little mill and farm service towns that dot Ontario's southwestern landscape. However, the main street still manages to exude vestiges of that long lost legacy.

This is most evident at the old courthouse square. It lies in the centre of the village at the corner of Brock St (the main street) and Lamport St.

Vittoria's former court house square is now the site of a church. The wood was made to look like stone.

The first building east of the square is the town hall built in 1879. The brick building boasts an unusual belfry. Today it houses a seniors' drop-in centre. Forming the southeast corner of Brock and Lamport is a large, grassy area. Here, by the street, stood one of the town's large block of stores. Known as the Lamport Block, it stood two storeys high and contained three stores. It was built in 1865 and demolished in 1965. Only the foundation remains.

A short distance south down Lamport Street a large church appears to be made of stone blocks. However, the construction material is in fact wood, designed to give a stone block effect. Standing on the spot where the old courthouse burned, it is today an Anglican church and was built in 1845.

On the north side of the main street, directly opposite the town hall, a two-storey brick building once housed a store and freight office, while the grand brick house immediately to its west is known as the Rebecca Anderson House. Built in 1851, it stands on property that had been in the Anderson family since 1802. The building is especially noted for the three French doors that open onto the front.

East on Brock St, the local general store occupies the village's oldest building, the former Catherwood hotel that dates from the days of the district capital. Murray St, which leads west from Lamport, presents an unusually large number of grand early homes for a village of this size, as does Brock St, west of the old square.

The overall image in Vittoria is one of lost grandeur, an image reinforced by the remaining buildings on the now quiet main street.

Directions

Vittoria is situated just west of Highway 24, about 10 kilometres south of the town of Simcoe.

 *Walkerville*

...the prettiest company town...

Although most "company" towns exhibit uniform, modest, and even cheaply built homes, Walkerville was deliberately intended as a model town, and the unusual beauty of its main street architecture conveys that intent.

It is all due to the town's founder, Hiram Walker. New England-born, he bought a pair of farms on the south shore of the Detroit River, where he opened a distillery.

In 1890 his eldest son, Edward Chandler, established the Walkerville Land and Building Company to create a "garden city." Here the wide and shady streets were lined with architect-designed homes.

While more modest workers' homes lay closer to the industrial section, the main street, Devonshire St, boasted Romanesque revival style homes for the company's management. Many of the grand homes were the work of Albert Kahn, the architect renowned for the magnificent Willistead mansion, the family castle. While the company's elaborate red stone office dominated the north end of the main street, Willistead anchored the south end.

It's hard to believe that the Florentine Renaissance brick building on the north side of Riverside Dr is a company office. The exterior displays long narrow Roman bricks, bronze gates and lanterns, while the interior contains mahogany and walnut panelling, Mexican onyx and Normandy and Egyptian marble. A garden on the river

This former hotel is one of many attractive structures on Walkerville's unusual main street.

side contains a sculpture fountain by A.N. DeLauro that depicts a First Nation motif.

A short distance west of the office, Devonshire St meets Riverside Dr where the town hall stands a short distance south on the east side. Designed by Kahn and built in 1904, it originally stood opposite the office, but was moved to this site in 1990 when it was threatened with demolition.

Beside the town hall stands the Crown Inn building. It was erected in 1893 to accommodate visitors arriving by rail. The old hotel rooms are now apartments, while the one-time office and dining room now house commercial businesses.

The next building seems out of step architecturally because it was once a post office, built in 1914, in the usual federal public works design. Opposite the post office, the tall pillared Bank of Commerce building is another design by the architect Kahn. This temple-like bank was built in 1907.

Lining both sides of the next block between Brant and Wyandotte Streets are six of the town's grander management homes. Those on the east side are semis and are noted for their arched porches. On the west side, number 511 is the former home of Thomas Reid, one-time head distiller who became Walkerville's first mayor. Built in 1898, the house displays a pillared porch and rounded tower. Next to it is number 547, the former home of John Bott, manager of the Walkerville Company, later to become the town's second mayor. Built in 1894, it is noted for its first and second floor porches and its many little turrets and dormers. Today it houses law offices.

The intersection of Devonshire and Wyandotte is marked by a pair of early commercial buildings, the Strathcona Building, a Kahn design from 1906, and immediately west of it the Imperial Building, which dates from 1922.

A string of handsome homes line the east side of Devonshire south of Wyandotte and represent the distinctive styles built to house Walker's managers. Those that formerly lined the west side were replaced with a bank building in 1922.

The block between Tuscarora and Cataraqui Streets shows more of the typical homes of Walkerville, most prominent of which is the McDougall-Stodgell House at number 712. It was built in 1915 by John A. McDougall, Secretary of Walker and Sons. Charles Stodgell, the next occupant, became yet another Walkerville mayor.

The most prominent building of the next block is "Foxley," once the home of Clayton Ambery, a private secretary in the Walker firm. This Tudoresque residence was built in 1906, another Kahn design, and was featured in American Architecture and Building News in 1910.

Here the main street takes a jog to the west around the "island"

At the south end of Walkerville's main street is the Willistead castle, the Walker family home.

occupied by St Mary's Anglican Church rectory and hall. Built in 1904, the English-style church was situated here to take advantage of the view down Devonshire Street to the river.

Along St Mary's Gate Street to the west of the church sits three of the town's grandest homes. Occupying the northwest corner of St Mary's Gate and Devonshire is the home built originally for Walker's grandson, Harrington E. Walker. Another grandson's home, that of Hiram H. Walker, formerly stood on the northeast corner.

Around the corner from St Mary's Gate, Kildare Road contains two more management homes. Marking the head of Kildare Rd stands one of Ontario's grandest castles, Willistead Manor. Surrounded by landscaped grounds of more than 15 acres, this sprawling Tudor style mansion was designed by Albert Kahn in 1906 and built for Hiram Walker's second son, Edward Chandler Walker. Leaded glass windows, clay tile roofs, and woodwork carved by Bohemian carvers all set this grand building apart. Nearby, the gatehouse and coach house both survive. Following the death of Walker's widow in 1921, the house and grounds became public property and variously housed the library, art gallery and council chambers. Today it is owned by the City of Windsor and is used for special events.

Walkerville's unusual main street offers a unique glimpse into a company town that set out to be the grandest company town in Ontario, and a stroll along its shady sidewalks confirms it succeeded.

Walkerville's main street can be found by following Wyandotte St west from Walker Road in the east end of Windsor. Walking tour information is available on the city's web site.

Directions

Walkerville lies in the east end of Windsor bounded by Riverside Dr to the north, Walker Rd to the east, Chilver to the west and Ottawa to the south.

 *Welland*

...more main street murals...

Welland has not enjoyed much luck in recent years. Industry has fled, and the main street resembles that of a ghost town where stores sit empty and heritage buildings have been abandoned. Yet the street still has one thing that invites visitors to linger—its incredible main street murals.

Many of these large wall paintings depict Welland's distinctive history, which dates back to the early years of one of Ontario's most ambitious engineering feats, the construction of the Welland Canal.

In 1829, when the canal opened, it was nowhere near Welland. Rather, it was built south from Port Dalhousie on Lake Ontario only as far as Port Robinson, where it followed the Welland River to Chippewa on the Niagara River. A few years later, in 1833, it was extended directly to Lake Erie at Port Colborne.

At many of the busy lock stations villages sprang up to house canal workers and lockmasters, along with taverns and accommodation for travellers. These evolved into today's communities of Port Dalhousie, St Catharines, Merritton, Allanburg, Port Robinson, Thorold and Welland. By the 1850s the railways arrived on the Niagara Peninsula and by the 1870s, Welland had become a railway hub. With its rail lines, canal, and cheap hydroelectric power, Welland attracted heavy industries. And in its heyday, its main street reflected that prosperity.

But eventually rail lines were abandoned, major highways bypassed the downtown core, and regional shopping centres and big box stores sprouted uncontrolled throughout the outlying areas. As they did, the downtown stagnated. Then, thanks in part to Canada's controversial free trade agreement, many of Welland's major industries downsized or closed outright.

To revitalize the main street, the city council commissioned more than two-dozen wall murals, an experiment which successfully revitalized the dying mill town of Chemainus, British Columbia.

Welland remained unlucky. While council initiated the murals, they failed to follow them up with other ways to draw people to the main street. The portion that lies east of the lift bridge remains a wasteland that lacks parks, cultural attractions, jobs, housing and even places to eat. Nor has there been any concerted effort at streetscape beautification or heritage preservation. Nearly a quarter of the stores sit empty. Yet, despite this, the amazing murals are an irresistible draw. In fact, no fewer than 16 lie either on or very close to East Main Street between King St and the railway tracks, just east of Burghar St.

A convenient and relevant starting point is at the junction of East Main and King Streets, by the now abandoned section of the Welland Canal and the lift bridge that rises above it. Look first at a pair of murals on King St itself, on the block just south of Main. Ironically, both depict street life on a once-busier Main Street. The artist of "Downtown Welland" on 14 King St is Toronto artist Phillip Woolf, while the mural on 22 King is by B.C. artist Mike Svob.

Walking east on Main, look above the bingo hall on the south side at 27 East Main, to see Ted Ziegler's portrayal of "Working Women" and the conditions they endured in Welland's 19th century facto-

Welland's railway heritage is depicted on this main street mural.

ries. As you come to Cross St, venture south a few paces to see Ron Baird's "Steam Engine" and Stefan Bell's "Tugboats," both of which portray Welland's vital transportation heritage.

Continue east along Main St, noting the historic town hall on the north side and the vacant lots where other heritage buildings once stood. At number 147 Lorraine Coskely-Black has depicted a collage of transportation, naming it "Where Water Meets Rail," also the name of a promotional hook used by the town itself in the 1920s to attract industry.

You'll need to look around the corner at Hellems St to see John Hoods' wall-sized depiction of the prestigious Welland Club.

The greatest concentration of murals lies on the next block close to Burghar St, where more than half a dozen lie. At number 188, on the north side of the street, a wonderful dusk impression of the now demolished Welland Junction railway station, with the pond in front of it, is entitled "The Pond... New Year's Eve", Ross Beard's work.

Then, on the south side, you will see a pair of works by renowned Chemainus artist Dan Sawatsky, "Little Helper" and "Tell Me About the Olden Days." The latter depicts the arrival of immigrants in Welland around 1910. Back on the north side, the painting on the side of number 212 by Marsha Charlebois shows one of Welland's most important founding industries, the Cordage Company, and in the parking lot beside it, John Hood's "Welland Fair."

One of the street's most striking murals is on the front of 228 Main. Titled "Upbound at Midnight" by Ross Beard, it is a dramatic night-time portrayal of an ocean freighter passing through the Welland Canal.

East of Burghar, the final pair of Main Street murals is found on number 285. Paul Elliot's "Triathlon" is a three-part piece depicting Welland's Mike Burwell participating in a gruelling tri-athlon. Finally, also on 285, Lambeth artist Risto Turunen shows school life in early Welland and is titled simply "Education".

Despite the appeal of the murals, there is little of architectural or historic significance on East Main St. The City of Welland Court House dates back to 1855, and was designed by leading Toronto architect Kiva Tully. The neo-classical structure displays four Ionic columns supporting a prominent gable; the roof is punctuated by three cupolas. A fire in 1913 destroyed much of Tully's interior work, and new extensions were added in 1954.

Close to the canal end of the street, numbers 20-26 comprise the Griffith Block, built as a commercial block of stores in 1876 and named for its owner, Thomas Griffith. The upper floor windows are rounded and capped with decorative keystones.

The most prominent structure on Main St, however, is not a building, but a bridge. The twin towers of the Welland Canal lift bridge,

Main Street's most prominent structure is the former life bridge across a now disused section of the Welland.

looming 170 feet (50 metres) into the air, are far higher than any other structure within view. It was built in 1927 to replace an earlier swing bridge over the fourth Welland Canal. When the latest Welland Canal bypass was completed in 1972, well to the east, the bridge was permanently lowered, ending the frequent traffic snarls that plagued the downtown area during ship passages.

The streetscape on the west side of the bridge remains less altered than that on East Main St, but the west side has only a single pair of murals. A number of early commercial buildings also line King St south of Main, but similarly boast only a few murals.

Directions

To reach Welland's main street murals, follow Highway 406 south from St Catharines to East Main St in Welland and follow it west. The murals begin just across the railway tracks.

 *Wroxeter*

...a ghost town no longer...

Around 1980, I visited the village of Wroxeter, and was astounded by the view. While some 18 stores and shops lined the two-block main street, built in the usual two-storey brick style, 15 were board-ed up. The sidewalks were cracked and weedy, and nobody was any-where on the silent roadway. Not too surprisingly, Wroxeter appeared in my ensuing volume of Ghost Towns of Ontario, not as a ghost town, but as one of Ontario's most completely ghosted main streets.

Happily, that description no longer applies. Struck by this label, the community rallied to reform its main street image. Old stores were removed and replaced with parkettes, new tenants were attracted, and the riverbanks were turned into landscaped parkland. Sidewalks were repaired and decorative streetlights installed. Then, to help celebrate the restoration of the street, an annual "ghost town" hoedown was initiated.

Today, the sign on the highway proudly announces Wroxeter as a "former ghost town."

A century ago however, the town thrived. Located at a waterpower site on the Maitland River, Wroxeter was first surveyed in 1847 and opened for settlement in 1854. In 1874 the Toronto Grey and Bruce Railway built a station near the town and business boomed. In the closing years of the 19th century the village could claim five hotels, five stores, four mills and a furniture factory. The main street was

Once boarded up, these main street stores in Wroxeter now have new tenants.

lined with nearly 20 places of business along with two churches and a school.

But the place still lacked the population necessary to achieve incorporated status as a village. That problem was solved when, during an unusually large influx of temporary workers, the census takers were called in and found enough "residents" to proclaim Wroxeter a real village. Later, in the 20th century, when the village found it could not finance hydro electricity, it was obliged to surrender this status.

Another problem faced by the town was that other nearby communities began to draw away business, especially to Wingham. Gradually, the stores closed their doors, and the main street fell silent, leaving it looking like the ultimate "ghost town."

Although that image has evaporated, Wroxeter's main street, Centre

St, is still quiet. The old downtown lies between the five points intersection at Centre and Anne Streets and the river. At the river, the grounds where the mills and factories once stood are now landscaped with a small lookout by the river, and the area goes by the name of Wroxeter Harbour.

The section of Centre St between the river and Queen St contained the greatest concentration of businesses. On the west side a Masonic Lodge, a post office, a variety of stores and the Mill Pond Restaurant now occupy the buildings. While the architecture is simple, the use of rounded windows on the two and three-storey buildings is typical of the era. Over on the east side, some of the old business premises have been removed completely, leaving a small parkette in their place.

South of Queen St, the main street is dominated by two churches and a community hall. At the southeast corner, the two-towered United Church dates from 1892; beside it is the community hall, likely an early school; immediately south of that is the simpler brick church, which dates from 1886.

On the west side of Centre, at the five points intersection, stands the former Estes Hotel. This two-storey brick structure features patterned brick arches over the Centre St windows, and no alteration to the ground level facade.

Many of Wroxeter's residential streets still contain the solid brick homes of a once-prosperous 19th century village. And they certainly have no ghosts.

Directions

 Wroxeter lies on Huron County Road 12 some 70 kilometres northwest of Kitchener.